How to Argue with an Economist

Second Edition

This fascinating book reflects on how economics is central to our lives, and how 'economic rationalism' has become the lens through which all Australian public life is viewed. It explains how this economic worldview overlooks important social issues, and how it transforms Australian culture.

In this second edition, Lindy Edwards further explores its continued influence on Australian culture. She argues that recent debates about industrial relations revolve around values, and the re-making of Australia's industrial relations system reflects a transformation in policymakers' worldviews and priorities.

How to Argue with an Economist equips a general audience to participate in these debates, exposing their pitfalls and values and making the issues accessible to everyone. These debates are about more than economics; they are about Australian society and culture in the generations to come.

Dr Lindy Edwards is Research Fellow at the Australian National University. She has worked as an economic adviser in the Department of Prime Minister and Cabinet, a political staffer, and a press gallery journalist.

Praise for the first edition
"This excellent book deserves to be widely read ... it sympathetically and seriously engages both economists and their critics ... combines passionate argument with generosity and fairmindedness."
Paul Oslington, University of New South Wales

How to Argue with an Economist

Second Edition

Reopening political debate in Australia

LINDY EDWARDS

CAMBRIDGE
UNIVERSITY PRESS

CAMBRIDGE UNIVERSITY PRESS
Cambridge, New York, Melbourne, Madrid, Cape Town, Singapore, São Paulo

Cambridge University Press
477 Williamstown Road, Port Melbourne, VIC 3207, Australia

Published in the United States of America by Cambridge University Press, New York

www.cambridge.org
Information on this title: www.cambridge.org/9780521699433

First published 2002
Second Edition 2007

Printed in Australia by Ligare Pty Ltd

A catalogue record for this publication is available from the British Library

National Library of Australia Cataloguing in Publication data

Edwards, Lindy.
 How to argue with an economist : re-opening political
 debate in Australia.
 2nd ed.
 Bibliography.
 Includes index.
 ISBN 9780521699433.

 1. Free enterprise - Australia. 2. Australia - Economic
 policy. 3. Australia - Politics and government – 1945- .
 I. Title.

 330.994

ISBN-13 978-0-52169-943-3 paperback
ISBN-10 0-521-69943-6 paperback

Cambridge University Press has no responsibility for
the persistence or accuracy of URLS for external or
third-party internet websites referred to in this publication
and does not guarantee that any content on such
websites is, or will remain, accurate or appropriate.

Contents

Part V The Future

Acknowledgements

Writing this book has been a wonderful experience and I want to express my gratitude to the wide range of people who have enthusiastically engaged with the ideas. The gamut of people who came out to argue on one side or the other has ranged from the usual suspects of political staffers, public servants and social science academics through to a broad sweep of people right across the country, from rural mums to corporate business leaders. It has been fantastic to draw such a wide range of people into these debates and I have appreciated the genuine engagement of them all.

I particularly want to acknowledge many senior members of the economics profession. They could have responded defensively but instead showed great openness, interest and enthusiasm. They have (rightly) treated the text as the critical reflections of someone within the profession. The many debates that have ensued have proved them well and truly worthy of the respect I hope the text conveys.

I would like to express my deepest gratitude to Darren Wright, my eternal rock and intellectual sparring partner, to Stephen Francis, my inspiration, and to Andrew Cleland, without whose belief this project would never have begun. To Fiona Reddaway who was there every step of the way with her drive, optimism and practical solutions. To Helen McLaren, Kirsten Andrews, Anna Wilson, Bruce Cohen, Jane O'Dwyer, Marco Salvio, Clive Hamilton, Ross Edwards (and those who asked not to be named) for their input to the fine tuning of the manuscript. To Glenn Withers and Michelle Grattan for creating the professional opportunities that enabled this book to come to fruition, to Ross Gittins without whose writing coaching the manuscript would have been unreadable, and to Peter Debus for picking up this project and running with it. To my colleagues at the Department of the Prime Minister and Cabinet who mentored, supported and taught me so much. To them, I want to emphasise that the criticisms in the following pages are intellectual and philosophical, but they have always had, and continue to have, my deepest respect. To Tracy Pateman who bore the worst of my stress at the most inopportune of times. She has carried the greatest burden of this process.

In putting together the second edition, I would particularly like to thank Barry Hindess, Frank Stillwell, Ian Marsh, Nick Gruen, Paul t'Hart, John Byron, Bob Gregory and Fred Argy for giving me their time and variously fuelling the intellectual fires in a variety of ways. I would like to thank Rod Rhodes and the Political Science Program in the Research School of the Social Sciences at the Australian National University for their collegiate company and accommodating me as a Visiting Fellow during the writing. I would also like to thank Kim Armitage and the team at Cambridge University Press for their ongoing support for the project.

Finally, I would like to thank Joo-Inn Chew, whose love and support makes all things possible.

Preface to the Second Edition

For political watchers interested in how our economy shapes our nation, its culture and values, the Howard years will go down as the great Australian drift.

Five years ago in the lead-up to the 2001 election I painted a picture of two political parties grappling for a vision. They were flailing around in the dark looking for a way to take Australia forward. There was a policy vacuum as a great chasm had opened up between the worldview of Canberra's policy elite and the electorate. There was a standoff between those who believed free markets were the only way forward and a wider public who simply did not share that view. It was not an argument, as the policy elites insisted, between the educated and the uneducated. It was a debate about values and worldviews.

The divide had begun with the economic reform era. A consensus emerged among the Canberra policy elite about how to reform the Australian economy. It was to slash tariffs, dismantle centralised wage fixing and float the currency. As the rhetoric of competition, free markets and efficiency rained down, it was not just economic policy that was being asked to change. The nation's old economic system, known as the Australian Settlement, had been the foundation of Australian culture. It was the basis of our unique egalitarian ethos, the cornerstone of the 'she'll be right' attitude, and what some call mateship. The essence of our culture was on the line, and many Australians did not want to see it slip away.

The divide sprang from a genuine battle of ideas. The principles of the reform era stemmed initially from a group of bureaucrats inspired by a branch of economics. The ideas spilled out of the bureaucracy and were embraced by policy elites, including both the major political parties. As the ideas spread they slipped from the social science of economics into the ideology of economic rationalism. A Canberra consensus emerged embracing a fully fledged worldview. At the same time the far-flung corners of the nation were still immersed in the attitudes of the Australian Settlement. They held onto fundamentally different views about the social dynamics of the nation. It was not a divide about technicalities or expertise, but about our fundamental beliefs about how our society works.

Five years ago John Howard was straddling the divide. He was caught between the views in the public service briefings and those he encountered on talkback radio. Howard supported free market reform but knew the electorate would not tolerate it. Ever the political pragmatist he side-stepped the debate. He meandered through his first terms in office before hitting on a new social agenda. He pushed into the culture wars and asserted a conservative sense of Australian identity. He kick-started rhetoric about the 'real Australians' and made theatre of cracking down on minorities and the disadvantaged. In the name of defending 'the Great Aussie Battler' he went to war against the 'Aboriginal industry', 'dole bludgers' and refugees he dubbed 'queue jumpers'.

In the years since, these underlying dynamics have remained the same. At the foundations, the policy stalemate has lingered on. Neither the government nor the opposition has a vision for economic reform that resonates with the electorate. The Howard government has inched slowly towards free markets, with the electorate recoiling at every step. To diffuse the conflict Howard has continued his strategy of distraction. He has managed the newspaper headlines by focusing on cultural identity and fuelling people's fears. The targets of the fear campaigns have changed. The stakes are higher and the strategies are more direct. But the basic political dynamic remains.

In preparing this second edition I was vexed by whether to update the whole text or to add new sections at the beginning and the end. I decided to keep the original text intact. It was an insider's account at the time it was written, and I wanted to hold onto that. Adding new chapters has the effect of charting our history. I was surprised when I looked back at the first edition to see how

Australia has changed. It is an opportunity to document the way we are moving through this nation-defining moment. As a result I have added this preface to bring the political context up to date and have added a new chapter at the end on industrial relations reform. I have touched up the final 'Making sure she'll be right' chapter to bring its discussions of the future into the current context. I have also added a box about economic efficiency and income distribution in the 'Arguing about efficiency chapter' to clarify my arguments about markets not being efficient if they are not just.

The more things change the more they stay the same

To bring the text forward to the present day it is useful to explore how things have changed and the ways they have stayed the same. Three major shifts can be seen to have transformed Australia's political landscape since the first edition.

A conservative Australia – Hanson and Al Qaeda

The bulk of the first edition of the book was written in the age of Pauline Hanson's One Nation Party and growing whispers about Asian immigration. Quiet discussion was slowly building around Australia's changing racial composition. There were early signs of a push away from the 1980s and 1990s embrace of multiculturalism and a return to ideas of a white Australia. But the discussion was covert. Critics attacked John Howard for his 'dog whistle' rhetoric. He used language that clearly appealed to a white Australia politics, but never said so directly. It was still not okay to attack someone directly because of their racial or cultural characteristics.

By 2006 Australian political debate had transformed. Concerns about Asian immigration had been swamped by a fear of Islam. The September 11 attacks in the USA had been whipped up into a fervor. Government campaigns warned people to be 'alert but not alarmed' and report 'anything suspicious'. Government Ministers began to talk about people needing to conform to 'Australian values'. In December 2005 when gang conflict went awry on a Sydney beach, talkback radio fuelled the fire. The Cronulla riots exploded, giving voice to racial tensions that had reached boiling point.

The magnitude of the shift in political debate was highlighted when Pauline Hanson embraced statements made by Federal Treasurer Peter Costello. Costello made a speech about Muslim beliefs and insisted that immigrants must conform to the values of their adopted country. Hanson embraced his view, but demanded recognition that he had come around to what she had been arguing all along. She said, 'I was crucified, I was ridiculed, I was called racist' for making similar comments only a few years before.

By 2006 the then Opposition Leader Kim Beazley was trying to outdo the government's cultural conservatism. He put forward proposals demanding immigrants sign up to a statement of Australian values. Australia has shifted from a place where it was unacceptable for a political leader to overtly attack people for cultural difference to one where neither of the major political parties dare not to. These days there are very few people at the centre of politics speaking the language of tolerance, inclusion and diversity.

Economic precariousness and the long boom

A second shift since the first edition has been the sustained economic boom. In 2002, memories of the 1990 recession were still vivid. There was a sense we'd only climbed out of the downturn recently, and that we could be thrown back into that uncertainty at any moment. The Asian currency crisis of 1997 had sent policy makers and the electorate into nervous anxiety. The dip of 2001 prompted a similar flurry. The sense of vulnerability was palpable. The fear of another recession threatened. But it was not to be.

Australia has now experienced 15 years of growth. The initial climb out of recession was kicked along by a housing boom. The First Home Buyer's Grant, introduced to soften the blow of the GST (the goods and services tax), helped spark an escalation in housing prices. As home owners watched their assets grow, they splurged on the credit card to celebrate. There was consumption and credit-fuelled frenzy. Australia's private debt levels reached dizzying heights. And just as we thought we had got as far we could on a no repayments plan, we got a further hand-up from the resources sector. Australia was plugged in to provide China with its natural resource needs. As China's economy leapt into the stratosphere so did we. We were spurred on for even further growth.

In 2006, the long shadow of the recession has almost vanished. Any economist knows the next recession will inevitably come. But after years of wondering whether this year might mark the end, we've started to discount doomsayers. Personal debt levels are at an all time high, and the nation's foreign debt needs breathing apparatus for the altitude. But we have come to take plentiful jobs and good times for granted. The spread of the economic spoils has been patchy. A severe drought, the persistence of long-term unemployment and the delayed take-up of young workers has meant the bounty has not been evenly shared. But while the government continues to parade around headline growth figures, these hardships are put down to personal failings. Australia has got relaxed and comfortable in a boom mentality.

Howard – From 'bumbling and visionless' to 'master statesman'

A final shift since the first edition is the transformation of the polling landscape. The first edition highlighted the volatility in the electorate. The voters had punished Keating with a resounding rejection in the 1996 election. Howard was thrust into office without an identifiable agenda. He meandered through his first term in office. He clung to gun control in the wake of the Port Arthur massacre to allow him to sneak back in 1998. In 2001, the electorate was in uproar over the introduction of the GST and looked set to eject Howard in the upcoming election. It was only as September 11 exploded into the world's consciousness that there was a sharp reversal in the polls.

In the years since, we've witnessed John Howard's elevation from 'visionless also-ran' to 'master statesman' and political strategist extraordinaire. Far from being volatile, the Howard government's hold on power seems impregnable. To political watchers on all sides of politics there has been growing belief that the top job is Howard's for as long as he wants it.

Howard's domination has been achieved through a masterful mixing of wealth and fear. As the economy has grown people's homes have expanded and television screens have widened. Australians have experienced a period of great wealth and are clinging to their comforts. But they have embraced a precarious safety as they have become fearful of what lies beyond the McMansion's gates. Those who have dared stick their head up have been assaulted with the politics of fear. Howard has alternated between the left jab of economic collapse and rising interest rates and the right jab of the terrorist threat. Punch-drunk and frightened most Australians have withdrawn into their heavily mortgaged homes.

Howard has become the leader who makes Australians feel safe. In the 2004 election he campaigned on 'trust' despite a number of scandals that exposed the slogan to ridicule. He knew that trust was a deeper issue. The boom of the 1950s and 1960s had created a confident, experimental generation that wanted to change the world. The boom of the 1990s–2000s created an inwardly focused generation of consumers, fearful of the world that lies outside. Australia has become a society that self-medicates its anxiety with retail therapy. And Howard has become its patron saint.

The continuities

These transformations make the Australia of 2002 feel a world away. Yet lingering beneath the surface there is also enormous continuity.

In June 1999, Prime Minister John Howard was quoted as stating that he did not believe greater government intervention in the economy was the way forward, but that the electorate would not tolerate government withdrawing. In 2006 he reiterated his commitment to free markets, declaring Margaret Thatcher and Ronald Regan to be his heroes, but continued to concede that the electorate does not support further free market reforms. He has been hamstrung by the schism. The last five years of his government reflect a political paralysis.

Economic policy has been largely in a holding pattern. Howard has had a few tilts at economic reform, but each has seen the electorate recoil. The GST and industrial relations both saw Howard nosedive in the polls. The government had to back down on the Snowy Hydro and postpone the sale of Medibank. They faced strong opposition to the sale of Telstra. The electorate's distaste is clear. But Howard still believes in free market policies, and inches towards them.

Labor has not offered a new injection of ideas either. Labor has been politically out-maneuvered in a way that has pilloried its political fortunes. The 1990 recession has hung like a lead necktie on each succeeding Labor leader. Their overwhelming failure in the public's eyes is that they are seen as having caused the 1990 recession. Their lack of economic credibility has made it hard to innovate and suggest alternate economic approaches. They have not dared err from the government's line for fear of being targeted as economic cowboys.

It has been a devastating shackle for the party. Their commitment to economic social justice built the bridge between their working class and latte socialist constituencies. They have not been prepared to campaign on the one issue that unites their supporters. As a result, they have fallen prey to divide and conquer tactics. Howard has systematically exploited the values divides between Labor constituencies. In the absence of being able to advocate its core values, the Labor Party has collapsed in a crisis of identity. To all and sundry it is no longer clear what they stand for.

For Australia, this has meant that there has been a policy drift for more than a decade. Economic settings have inched in the same directions as the reform era. But they have done so ever so slowly. There have been more privatisations, the slow and half-hearted continuation of competition policy, and the definitive end of the wage arbitration system through new workplace laws. Yet, to a remarkable degree the policy drift has meandered on.

Economic challenges on the horizon

The long boom has buffered any impetus for an economic re-think. If the economy had been in the doldrums there would have been more pressure for action. Governments would have needed to sell economic ideas that appealed to the electorate. They would have been forced to tackle the divide head on. So far the trappings of prosperity have enabled the debate to be shuffled to the back-burner. But that may be about to change.

The economic storm clouds are brewing. While the headline growth rates are strong, the story on the ground is increasingly patchy. The bubble boom was fuelled by consumer debt and there are few emerging industries to pay the bills. For the moment the official numbers are being held up by the Western Australian and Queensland resources sectors. But things have started to falter in the south-eastern states. Droughts, interest rate rises and petrol prices are putting households under pressure. The over-indulged credit cards and mortgages are getting harder to manage. Bankruptcies are on the rise.

The economy is also still burdened by the fallout of the reform era. Much has been made of the escalating fortunes of the rich. But it is the picture at the bottom end that is most disturbing. The economic restructuring between the 1970s and 2000 saw the proportion of working-aged men in full-time jobs drop a stunning 20%, from about 87% to only 67%. Some of these men are in education, others in part-time work, but many have ended up on some form of welfare. When all the different types of benefits are combined, nearly 20% of working-age Australians rely on government benefits. The years of growth have made remarkably little inroads into what has become an entrenched underclass.

As the boom crumbles the major parties will be sent scurrying for solutions. They will need to put together an economic strategy that appeals to the public. Ideas about the economy will burst back onto the political agenda. The challenge will be to put together a vision that addresses the major problems of our times, while still acknowledging the role of our economy in shaping our culture and values.

It is not enough for an economy to deliver headline growth statistics. The aggregate numbers are only part of the picture. Sitting below the numbers are communities, businesses and workplaces. Economic relationships make up the bulk of our social relationships. The jobs we do, where we work and how we relate make up the essence of our day-to-day lives. The economy is not separate from the social system. It is an integral part of a culture and a way of life.

The Australian Settlement was one of the cornerstones of Australian culture. The Settlement was not perfect. Nonetheless, as an economic strategy it shaped our view of the world. We lived in a society where the community made decisions about how they wanted to live and set about organising an economy that could deliver it. It embodied our belief that we can come together and collectively manage ourselves. It was a manifestation of our assumption that we can author our own communities.

The Settlement also underpinned our unique blend of individualism and egalitarianism. The ethos of ensuring no one fell too far behind contributed a sense of we are all in this together. The collective commitment to equality (at least amongst white men) created a culture in which people saw one another as allies. It built a culture of social trust. It has generated a sense of safety that permeates our communities so completely we only acknowledge it when we quip that 'she'll be right'.

The era of market reform challenged that culture. We had years of being bombarded with rhetoric of government relinquishing control to the market. We were told that governments are slow, cumbersome and ineffective, and that free markets do a better job. That democratic government could not withstand the global forces of capital flows. That government is weak and inefficient relative to the mighty power of the market. The message was loud and clear. We did not have control over our collective lives anymore.

We were also told to relinquish the ethos of egalitarianism. The commitment to full employment and arbitrated wage fixing was abandoned. As Australia transformed from one of the most equal societies in the western world to one of the least, we faced changing our national character. As high-income earners race ahead while large chunks of the population languish as long-term unemployed, it changes our relationships to one another. As some become comfortable in a world of abundance while others skip from one low-paid casual job to another, it undermines our shared experience. Social solidarity is threatened and we risk becoming a different people.

As Australia comes out of the long boom we will have to re-imagine ourselves. We will have a choice about whether we find new ways forward that hold on to the old ideals of the Australian Settlement. Or whether we continue with the directions of the reform era and accept the cultural change that will bring.

We will be re-thinking our future in a new context. The post-September 11 era has seen the re-birth of the strong state. Federal governments have stepped forward and re-taken their place as protector of the nation. It remains to be seen whether that will extend to protecting communities from other global forces. We will also be facing new challenges, many of which are also confronting others around the world. There will be the response to climate change as the international community moves to cut carbon emissions. The technological revolution has also created economic schisms in many advanced democracies. It has rendered the unskilled unemployable while the highly skilled have raced on to higher and higher wages. Australia will have a choice about whether we import other countries' solutions to these problems. Or whether we dream up some of our own that are more in line with our traditions.

As we undertake this new journey understanding economic rationalist ideas will be as important as ever. There will be a national debate to be had about the role of markets and our ability to shape and constrain them. It will be essential to understand both the strengths of free market ideas and the values and beliefs behind them. My intention in writing this book was to equip people to participate in such debates no matter which side you are on. I hope you find it a lively introduction to some of the major philosophical and political debates of our time.

Part I

A Historical Juncture

Chapter 1

A political impasse

'How lucky can you get. They were down for the count. They had no idea what they were going to do. Then "pewft" – September 11. And they've got it on a platter.' The 30-something Labor hack stretched back on the couch and laughed in macho nonchalant fashion. Like so many of the Labor boys when reality bites too hard, he retreated behind the cynical veneer. At the popular Canberra pub, the motley crew of political insiders – bureaucrats, journos and political staffers – stared into their beers and contemplated the chips selection.

After a few moments another staffer broke the silence. 'I can't think about it that way. I can't believe it was an accident of circumstance and line up to do it all again.' She pursed her lips. 'The bottom-line is our vote was soft. We had a big lead in the two-party preferred in February. But the polls swung wildly because people weren't committed to us. We were vulnerable because we hadn't tapped into what people wanted.'

In a sea of outrage, bafflement and disappointment, political watchers of all colours and creeds are scrambling to make sense of the 2001 federal election. Steeped in fear and xenophobia, the campaign has been dubbed one of the lowest ebbs in Australian political history. But a common theme is emerging in the post-mortems. It is not the insecure and anxious electorate. Or even the conservatism of both leaders. The common theme is the policy vacuum.

The campaign's policy pickings were meagre. Both sides' desperate scramble for election ideas had amounted to zip. The incumbent Coalition had little to offer. Policy launch upon policy launch announced things they had already done, and programs already in train. Labor was struggling to come up with a post-Keating agenda. They had settled for a Whitlamesque approach to jobs, education and health. But they were fiddling at the margins rather than sweeping reforms. Both sides had hit a brick wall. Neither side had any solutions.

As the creative capacities of our political elite stalled, they opened a space for the campaign that followed. In an absence of answers, debate was diverted. Unable to offer people their hopes, John Howard settled for focusing their fears. As his rhetoric zeroed in on the dark corners of the Australian psyche, debate shifted from our ambitions to our anxieties. We became swamped by threats rather than elevated by opportunities. And Labor offered no respite.

As Australia looks for answers to the current political mood, we have to look to the policy drift.

The policy drift

The current policy drift is the dead patch at the change of the tide. Australia is on the cusp of a new political era. The old era is dead and both sides of politics are grappling for a new way forward. The economic rationalist reform agenda initiated by the Labor government and continued by the Coalition is completed. The implementation of the GST (the goods and services tax) was the last instalment. For the first time in years, both sides of politics are in search of a new direction.

As the parties flail around in the darkness, their compasses have gone haywire. The old indicators of left and right have vanished and a great divide has blocked the only way forward. The divide is not between the city and the bush or between Labor and Liberal. It is a growing divide between the Australian people and their policy makers. Economic rationalism is the flashpoint, but it is not an argument about the economy. It is a mismatch of values and priorities.

On the one hand is a public fed up with economic rationalism. After 20 years of reform and the best part of a decade of the promised growth, people do not believe that economics is going to deliver the community they want to live in. And on the other is an administrative elite in which the economic orthodoxy charges on unquestioned. Politicians have been left straddling the divide, paralysed as the ground is swallowed beneath them. They desperately need a way forward but the two views seem irreconcilable.

Economic rationalism

'Economic rationalism' is the label slapped on a set of ideas that gripped Australian public policy circles through the 1980s and 1990s. Some people use the term to describe putting economic considerations above other values. Others use it to describe an ideological commitment to small government and free markets. My use of the term incorporates both of the above. In Chapter 5 I will outline in detail the ideas I am defining as economic rationalism. The ideas are a simplification of neo-classical economics that combine to yield a worldview.

They are adrift in the gulf between our professional policy makers and their public.

The public mood

The current malaise has been building for nearly a decade. In the mid 1990s reports of public discontent were flowing into both political parties. Backbenchers recounted anecdotes of the bitter public mood. People were fed up. They complained they were losing their communities and their way of life. In the lead-up to the 1996 election Liberal Party research found that people felt they were being ignored. People said 'Canberra' was not recognising their priorities and had no empathy with their problems. Newspaper polling found that almost a half of Australians planned to vote for the party they disliked least. People were not drawn to the parties' visions and did not associate with their values.

When Pauline Hanson sprang onto the scene she shocked the political establishment into realising it had a crisis on its hands. She was swept to prominence when she won the regional Queensland seat of Oxley. An unknown Liberal candidate in a safe Labor seat, she was thrown into the limelight on racism. She had written an anti-Aboriginal letter to her local paper. When the incident got national publicity, Coalition Leader John Howard had to expel her from the party to prove his own questionable race credentials to the big southern electorates. In the flood of publicity that followed,

Hanson, a political novice with little education, emerged as some-one who shared the views of many disenfranchised Australians and who wasn't afraid to speak her mind. She provided a vent for the electorate's frustration. She was swept to power as an independent, winning the largest swing in the nation.

Hanson set up her own political party, One Nation, and ignited Australian politics. While racism fuelled her notoriety, her speeches connected with a lot of Australians:

> The only employment growth has been in part time and casual jobs, and those Australians lucky enough to have a full time job have to work longer and longer to keep their families' heads above water. The eight hour day is a thing of the past. Growth in low skilled and low paid part time and casual jobs is a worrying trend. It is not possible to raise a family or pay off a home on such an insecure and paltry income, and irregular and inconsistent work hours make family life very difficult.

> Successive Liberal and Labor governments, including this current group of treacherous self seekers, have worked for the interests of just about everyone except the Australian people who elected them and pay them. (Pauline Hanson, Parliament House, Hansard)

In 1997 One Nation won 11 seats in the Queensland election. It was one of the most successful results ever for a new political party. Most of the seats had been snatched from the Liberal and National parties. Party polling indicated the National Party was at risk of being almost entirely rubbed out in the upcoming federal election.

Parliament House was in a flurry as the major parties realised the magnitude of the public crisis of confidence. There were panicked meetings around the halls of Parliament House. Analyses of the Hanson phenomenon attributed some of her success to racism, but most of it was about giving the big boys a kick. People were sick of not being listened to. They were fed up with the economic agenda that marched forward irrespective of their views. They had had enough of watching their lives being eroded and being powerless to do anything about it. Labor started to back away from its economic rationalist rhetoric and Prime Minister Howard moved to tell people that he 'understood' their concerns.

In 1998 the major parties closed ranks to quash the uprising. They teamed up to do a preference swap and eject Hanson from federal politics. Liberal Cameron Thompson ousted Hanson despite having received just over half of her primary vote. Preference deals also kept One Nation's representation in the Senate to a minimum. But, despite what can only be described as a chaotic and unprofessional campaign, One Nation won 9% of the national primary vote. Again, a spectacular performance for a new political party.

In its second term the Howard government took a sharp turn to the right. Ignoring Hanson's economic policy concerns it took up her mantle of social intolerance. It made sport of beating up on minority groups. Policies affecting handfuls of people were blown up into national issues. There were media frenzies over illegal immigrants, welfare cheats and in-vitro fertilisation for lesbians. The cunning strategy enabled the government to voice its intolerance without hitting too many potential voters. But it wasn't enough. The economic reform program rolled on and people continued to be angry. As the government entered the election year it continued to slip in the polls.

The rise and rise of economic rationalists

The electorate had hoped that the gulf between government aspiration and the public's concerns would be overcome when Labor Prime Minister Paul Keating was bundled out of office in 1996. Keating had been attacked for being arrogant, aloof and out of touch with the average Australian. He was widely held as being responsible for the economic reform agenda, and the electorate relished giving him a good solid kick in the 1996 election. He was thrown out in a landslide defeat for Labor, losing 31 seats.

But, far from easing the economic rationalist clout, the change of government served to exacerbate it. Despite the signs of a political moodswing, the change of government boosted economists' power within the bureaucracy. After the 1996 election, under the guise of clearing out 'Labor hacks', a program of workplace renewal began. In the powerful Department of the Prime Minister and Cabinet, people with non-economic backgrounds and a broader social perspective were deemed to be lefties and were replaced by narrow economists. Longstanding department members groaned under the weight of what they called 'the Treasury invasion'. Economists from economic rationalist establishments like the Productivity Commission even began appearing at the lower levels in the social policy areas.

Within a couple of years the impact on the department was evident. In May 1998 the Howard government brought down its third round of harsh budget cuts. Publicly the government was being condemned by opposition parties for a policy akin to 'starving the children to pay the mortgage'. But within the department the mood was strangely consensual. Traditionally, the department's social, economic and industry divisions were recruited from the respective social, economic and industry departments. The different departments' cultures and political bents usually made the annual post-budget presentation a fiery affair. But that year the debate was silent. People filed in, listened to the presentation and asked a few non-controversial questions. Efforts to spark debate about the social justice of the budget strategy were met with a polite silence. As people slunk out of the room the old hands were uneasy about the new consensus.

The trend is evident across the public service. Even as school leavers turn away from economics degrees, bureaucrats continue to flock to economics courses at the Australian National University or the University of Canberra. They believe their careers hit a ceiling if they do not have economics qualifications. In 1999 the Canberra branch of the Economics Society was the only branch across Australia to report a strengthening membership. And when asked about what new paradigm will replace economic rationalism, most young bureaucrats return blank looks. A change is not on their horizon. They insist that economics is the only way of analysing the issues facing government.

Straddling the divide

Politics is where the two worldviews collide. The politicians have the policy elite in their ear on the one hand and the public on the other and they have been forced to bridge the gap between the two. In June 1999 in an interview with the *Australian*, the Prime Minister captured the quandary his government was caught in. Howard said that, although he did not think more government involvement was the answer to Australia's problems, 'the community won't accept government withdrawing'. He was caught in the crosscurrent. The ideas and policy prescriptions taken for granted by the policy elite were unacceptable to the electorate. A gulf had emerged between the values the Prime Minister encountered on talkback radio and the values underlying the public service briefings he read each day.

Amidst a storm of criticism about its lack of vision the Howard government bluffed its way through its first term, clinging to gun control and tax reform as proof it was going somewhere. Finally, part way through its second term the government found a way to straddle the divide. Howard found a way to articulate a vision that bridged the gap. In a landmark speech to the Australia Unlimited Roundtable, the Prime Minister talked about the two complementary policy approaches of market liberalism and 'modern' conservatism. He argued that market liberalism was fundamental to engaging with the global economy and consistent with the liberal traditions of the party. But, he said, Australians needed to be cushioned through this process of change. The stresses of change were exacting a greater cost from some parts of the community than others. He argued that it was consistent with the conservative element of the party's tradition to provide an 'anchor' to people through this time of rapid change. The government had a role to 'minimise the impact of these outcomes and provide positive alternatives' for those struggling with the changes.

John Howard's speech had an eerie echo of Paul Keating's 1993 victory speech. After winning the 1993 election Keating made an appeal to the 'true believers'. He said that economic liberalisation was inevitable in embracing the modern age. The difference, he said, between Labor and the Coalition was that Labor would reach back and lift up those who were being left behind. It would cushion the blow for the hardest hit and the least able to cope with change.

After four years in office the Coalition had reached the same conclusion Labor had reached six years before. Being a social progressive was identical to being a liberal conservative. Both amount to a commitment to free markets, with a caring eye to those suffering through the transition. To the extent that there is any view of how to move forward, both parties had come to the same conclusion: that the policy elite in Canberra were right, and that the punters just didn't understand. Both sides had concluded that the public were battered, bewildered and didn't realise it was all for their own good. Both sides talked endlessly about needing to 'explain' things better to the electorate.

While there was a vision of how to move forward, the divide was sustainable. The politicians knew where they were going and they had something to talk about. Both Labor and Liberal became immersed in the 'politics of economic necessity'. They rammed through wave after wave of economic reform on the basis that we had no choice. They talked about 'banana republics', 'the recession we had to have', and 'buffers against the Asian crisis'. They wheeled out experts and saturated the electorate in jargon, graphs and numbers to give a scientific credibility to the unpopular reforms. Governments led and, with only a choice between 'Tweedledum and Tweedledee', the voters had no choice but to follow.

The tensions are being pushed to a climax because the economic liberalisation agenda is complete. When Paul Keating began the economic reform process as Labor Treasurer, five pillars of economic reform were identified: floating the currency and freeing up the financial system, slashing tariffs, cutting back the government sector, ending centralised wage fixing, and tax reform. With the Howard government's implementation of tax reform, both parties have been sent scrambling to find a new vision, a new agenda to take Australia into the 21st century. As the politicians grapple for something new, something to grab the hearts and minds of Australians, the divide is harder to ignore. It presents an impasse.

However, this is not simply a debate between an educated intelligentsia and 'punters' who just don't understand. It is a debate about values. Australia is at a historical turning-point. How we resolve this divide will shape the character of the nation over the next century.

Chapter 2

A nation-defining choice

Bridging the divide and reacquainting our policy makers with their public is not just a matter of solving a temporary political impasse. It is more than a problem to patch over. How Australia goes about bridging the divide between the electorate and the policy circles will be pivotal in shaping its ongoing culture and values. The economic rationalist reform period was a revolution that changed more than our economy. As this period of change comes to a close, our response to it will set the foundations of the Australia of the 21st century.

Things to be put to one side

The fabric of a national culture is woven together by thousands of different threads. How we organise our economy is an important, even foundational, thread, but it is not the only thread that runs through Australian culture. Through the economic rationalist years there has been a bundle of grand-scale cultural changes that aren't closely related to economic policy and aren't the focus of this book. These have included the rise of feminism, multiculturalism, Aboriginal reconciliation, environmentalism and gay rights. These movements have all impacted, in different ways, on our ideas about what it is to be an Australian. But while recognising their importance I will leave those changes to be discussed by others. My purpose is to draw out the largely under-recognised thread of the impact of economic changes on our culture.

Australia's economic transition

Casting an eye over world trends in the 1980s, it's easy to make the mistake of believing that Australia's dalliance with economic rationalism was just a political fad. The British and the Americans had their own versions. Thatcherism and Reaganomics, as they came to be known, dominated the political landscapes of Australia's two greatest allies. Our policies could be mistaken for merely keeping abreast of international fashions or wanting to keep in line with our allies. But while international intellectual fashions were not an irrelevant part of the story, Australians had often taken great pride in spurning British and American policy prescriptions in the past. International fashions were not what sparked it all, and the consequences will run much deeper than a fad.

In the years between Federation and the 1970s Australia developed a unique social and economic compact. The compact has become known as the 'Australian Settlement'. An egalitarian spirit combined with a post-Federation fervour to populate this vast continent, giving rise to a uniquely Australian vision. We set about building a workers' paradise. Our leaders aimed to offer plenty of jobs, good wages and a high standard of living to the country's workers. In doing so they would lure new immigrants from across the waters. Meanwhile the egalitarian society would give the many Australians of humble origins a great opportunity. The new nation was to be based on the principles of equality and a fair go. Working people would come to Australia for a better chance at life.

An economic strategy evolved to deliver this workers' paradise. The arrangement was that industries would be protected if they paid high wages. Manufacturing industries developed in urban areas to provide jobs. The industries were required by law to pay high wages. The minimum wage was legislated to be enough for a man to support his family. Industrial relations arbitration was established to smooth out conflict between workers and bosses. Arbitrations were made about wages on the basis of what was required to give workers a good standard of living. Over the years as prosperity increased and expectations about a 'reasonable' standard of living grew, the minimum wage rose accordingly.

To survive in this high wage environment, industries had to be protected. Large tariff barriers were erected. The infant manufacturing industries were protected from international competition from lower wage countries. The tariffs (taxes on goods being imported) kept the prices of imports high, enabling Australian products to be competitive with imports despite Australia's high cost structures. It enabled Australian manufacturing industries to stay afloat despite paying high wages. Investment flowed into the protected industries as governments effectively guaranteed them a profit. The industries flourished. In the post-war period Australia's 'long boom' yielded high wages and 1–2% unemployment.

However, the Australian Settlement social compact had its costs. It had serious consequences for the balance of trade (i.e. the balance between exports and imports). Australia imported a lot of the consumer items that underpinned its high standard of living. It also had to import a lot of the capital equipment for its manufacturing industries. These imports were expensive and had to be paid for. But the manufacturing industries were high cost and could not compete internationally to sell their wares. Up until the 1950s manufactures were never more than 6% of Australia's exports. The arrangement was not self-sustaining. The primary industries sector stepped into the breach.

In the first half of the century, the boom in agriculture and wool was the nation's saviour. Australia's primary industries were some of the best in the world. Internationally wool and agricultural products were attracting good prices and were exported in large quantities. They earned valuable foreign exchange that could be used to pay the country's bills. Imports could be paid for, there was money in the government coffers, and the urban manufacturing 'quality of life industries' could be sustained.

In the 1960s Australia's fortunes were again propped up by the primary sector. There was a boom in the minerals industry. The post-war growth in Europe, Japan and North America boosted world mineral prices. Australia found a number of rich deposits, and coal, iron ore and bauxite became its new leading exports. Again the primary industry sector propped up the nation and paid its import bills, underwriting the social contract that was providing the Australian way of life.

By the 1970s, however, it was all falling apart. The primary industries were facing declining terms of trade. All over the world, prices for agricultural products were falling. The prices we were receiving for our exports were dropping. At the same time the cost of our imports was climbing. The post-war boom had upped the standard of living around the world. Australians wanted televisions, washing machines and cars. Our import bill was climbing just at the time our ability to pay for it was going backwards.

The problem was compounded because some business sectors had become lazy behind the tariff walls. They had focused their efforts on lobbying governments to increase protection rather than on improving the efficiency of their industries. The tariff protection was insulating them not just against high wages, but also against inefficient business practices. The efforts to sustain the manufacturing sector became an increasing drain on the economy, but the primary sectors could not plug the hole anymore. The arrangement had lasted three quarters of a century but time had run out. It could not be sustained any longer. Our economy was in crisis and something had to be done.

That was the context when the Hawke–Keating government kicked off the program of economic rationalism in the early 1980s. Arguably it was not the only course of action available. But economic liberalism was on the rise in the USA and the UK, where many Australian economists were educated. It was the obvious choice. As Treasurer, future Prime Minister Paul Keating seized the initiative. He latched on to the fashion of the moment, was educated in its ways and became its champion. In 1987 he was declared the *Economist*'s International Finance Minister of the Year for his hard-headed commitment to bringing economic reform to Australia.

Over the next 20 years, free market liberalism came to permeate the nation's economic policy. Australia went from being one of the most protected economies in the world to one of the least. Centralised wage fixing was all but abandoned and the industrial relations system was overhauled. The financial system was thrown open and the currency floated. Government services were rationalised, privatised and put out to competitive tendering. The final stage of the economic rationalist reform program was tax reform. It was introduced in July 2000.

Not just an economic change

The first half of this book argues that the economic reform process was not just an economic change. The Australian Settlement had embodied the values of the nation. The ideals of the workers' paradise were enmeshed in the values of quality of life for all and a fair go. The free market liberalism that underpinned the new economic arrangements also embodied a new set of values. Economic policies that were supposed to be mere tools in tackling a specific crisis cut to the core of the Australian character. They tore down institutions the society was based on. They discarded time-honoured ways of doing things and shattered the way in which Australians thought about each other and their place in the world. In the 1980s Australians were told they lived in a dog-eat-dog world where they had to struggle against one another to survive. In the national rhetoric, quality of life was replaced with economic efficiency, security became a competitive edge, and a fair go became a knockdown drag-out affair.

The economic reform program undermined Australia's commitment to equality. The commitment to full employment and high real wages was abandoned in the drive to liberalisation. Real wages declined and the divide between the haves and the have-nots widened. Professor Anne Harding from the National Centre for Social and Economic Modelling found that wages polarised. The number of workers clumped around the middle (median) of the wage income distribution decreased sharply. About two-thirds of them slipped behind, while one-third raced ahead. The bottom 50% of Australians lost ground as their share of the nation's wealth dropped. The gains went primarily to the wealthiest 10%, who increased their share of the nation's wealth from 23% to 26% in the decade between 1982 and 1993–94.

The Labor government tried to cushion the blow on its working class constituency by increasing what it called the 'social wage'. The social wage included government-funded family assistance, Medicare, childcare and education support. It was targeted at the least well off. As people's jobs and wages dropped away, government provided services to prop up their quality of life.

However, the Labor government did not anticipate that the social wage would change the culture of equality. A social stigma was attached to 'dole bludgers'. Middle income earners began to resent the 'hand-outs'. The payments help focused on those at the very bottom. The result was that during the 1980s the rich were getting richer, the poorest were getting a hand up from government (which left them staying about the same), but those in the middle were losing ground. Middle income earners were frustrated about being excluded from support targeted at the lowest income groups. They became angry that no one was preserving their position in the world, and the downwards envy that Pauline Hanson captured so effectively emerged.

The policy of putting the reform agenda before employment meant low-income people were deprived of the dignity of a job, of providing for their families and feeling that they had earned their keep. Scores of families had no breadwinner. The pool of the long-term unemployed continued to deepen as ghettos of entire unemployed communities began to emerge. People got stuck in poverty traps and physically or psychologically could not get out of them. Both sides of politics started to talk about the problems of welfare dependence.

During this reform period, for the first time in generations, young people grew up knowing they would have to struggle for a job. Their futures were not secure and they would have to claw their way past their peers to get a place in society. Even as the economy began to grow, the sense of precariousness remind. Drenched in the mindset of competitiveness many extended their work hours to stay ahead of the pack.

Australians' sense of confidence and safety had been shattered. No longer confident that 'she'll be right', there was a push for a crackdown on law and order. The New South Wales state elections in the late 1990s were dominated by the issue. Australians had started to lose their trust in one another. They no longer felt safe in their homes. Government promised more police and tougher penalties for offenders. They talked about being tough on crime and restoring order on the streets.

In 1997, despite four years of economic growth, a survey by the Australia Institute found that only 13% of Australians thought quality of life was improving and about half that it was declining. It showed that there was a vast gulf between economic performance and public opinion about Australian society and the direction of change. In June 1999 social researcher Hugh Mackay in his *Mind and Mood of Australia* report found that Australians felt there was too much emphasis on economic growth and it was coming at the cost of quality of life.

In 1999 the Republic Referendum dragged Australia's fractured sense of identity into the spotlight. The Republicans tried to base their campaign on a call to national pride. But they floundered. They shied away from talking about what it is to be an Australian. They could not enunciate it, and did not try. For nearly 20 years international competitiveness was all our leaders had talked about. But not many Australians felt international competitiveness was worthy of celebration. Most still held a deep commitment to the values of quality of life and a fair go. It would have felt hypocritical to celebrate the values at a time we feel we are betraying them. Australia's centenary was not a time of standing up and being proud of Australian values. It was a time of watching them slip away.

The challenge

The economic rationalist reform era created a gulf between the Australian people's values and how their society actually operated. The imported solution to our economic crisis ran against the grain of our national fabric. Policies that had sat relatively comfortably with the American and British political traditions did not fit in Australia. To fix an economic crisis, Australians were asked to stop being who they were.

It is this gulf that is now playing itself out in Australia's political quandary. On the one hand Canberra's policy circles have reached a consensus that the economic rationalist route is the only option open to Australia. This view has come to permeate all centres of power. Initially under Keating and again under Howard, those institutions that advocated the economic rationalist vision were bolstered while those that questioned it were sidelined. Those with the right economic credentials were promoted and those without them stood by as they were leap-frogged by young up-and-comers with the 'correct' worldview. There are still many people who do not advocate the economic rationalist worldview, but the positions of authority are monopolised by those who do.

By contrast, the community is still steeped in the values of quality of life for all. Community values take longer to change than intellectual fashions. People still dream of the workers' paradise (though their belief it can be delivered has been eroded) and they maintain a commitment to a fair go. Organisers of the Olympics were caught out by how strong this sentiment still is in Australia. There was a public uproar about the sale of tickets to the Games. The public was outraged that the best seats were being sold exclusively to the rich at exorbitant prices. They resented that not more of the seats were available in the public ballot, where people nominated for relatively inexpensive tickets and everyone had an equal chance of winning them. They were committed to equality of access for all to 'the people's games'. The uproar would not have occurred in a lot of countries.

Canberra's inner circles have missed this gulf in values. They have mistakenly attributed the electorate's resistance to economic reform as being solely about the pain of economic change. They have noted the increasing trend of people cutting ties with political parties. They accept that Australian politics will be increasingly marred by electorates seeking to punish governments with wild angry swings as people lodge protest votes against whichever party is in power. But there is little recognition that people are angry because no one is representing their values. No one is promising the things people actually want.

The Coalition has twigged that people are feeling ignored and misunderstood. It crafted its victorious 1996 election campaign around telling people 'we understand'. But its strategy was to tell people it understood their anger. Liberal Party polling revealed people's frustration at watching their social standing slipping while the government helped out others. The Coalition captured the 'what about me?' sentiment. It cunningly devised the campaign slogan: 'For all of us'. In its first term in office it made theatre of cracking down on the unemployed, Aborigines, immigration and minority groups. Unable to demonstrate any understanding of people's aspirations, it settled for showing an understanding of their vices.

But that is a short-term solution.

Conclusion

The current political impasse is a symptom that we are at a historical juncture in a debate about Australian values. The uproar about economic rationalism is a conflict over the kind of community Australia wants to be. The way we arrange our economy is deeply intertwined with our culture, and the economic policies we pursue in the aftermath of the economic rationalist reform period will shape our nation into the next century.

But, to date, we have been struggling to have these debates. Critiques of economic rationalism have been flowing for over a decade to no avail. Economic rationalism remains unshakeably incumbent. To find the way forward it is necessary to understand why.

Chapter 3

Economic rationalism's grip on power

To tackle economic rationalism we need to understand how it got its grip on government and why. We need to understand the roots of its power, how it influences decision making and why it continues to be powerful despite the community outcry. It is often claimed that economic rationalism is driven by a small group of powerful vested interests. That behind a cloak of secrecy, powerful business interests are controlling the agenda. But the conspiracy theories are misplaced. The reality is less sinister and more difficult. To understand its stranglehold on power, and to tackle it effectively, it is necessary to understand the black box of government. We need to understand how decisions get made and why economic rationalism is so dominating.

How governments make decisions

The way governments make decisions is an imprecise science. The entangled interactions of the bureaucracy, politicians and lobby groups pump out hundreds of decisions a week. Which of the three groups has the upper hand in any decision depends on the issue. The bulk of government decisions are bureaucracy led. That is, the bureaucracy will tell the politicians there is a problem, devise a plan to fix it and ask to be authorised to do the job. The politicians usually agree. Sometimes the politician will have a personal view on the issue and over-ride the bureaucrats. At other times lobby groups will get in the politician's ear and convince them to take a different approach. But with the vast majority of issues, particularly smaller ones, the politicians accept that the bureaucracy are the experts and do as they suggest.

A smaller number of normally very important issues tend to be politician led. That is, the politicians will go to the bureaucracy and explain an outcome they want and ask the bureaucracy to work out how to do it. These ideas normally come from within the political parties themselves. They are often developed through extensive discussions with lobby groups and affected parties. Or at least the good ones are. Occasionally some bright spark will have an idea in a taxi on the way to a meeting, leaving bureaucrats and political staffers alike cleaning up the debris for months.

The relationships between bureaucrats and politicians are usually tense. Most commonly bureaucrats see themselves as protecting the community from the politicians. They fear the politicians' schemes are harebrained and impractical at best, or driven by marginal seat politics and a desire for personal grandeur at worst. Politician-led policies are often greeted with a roll of the eyes and a groan as the bureaucrats shift into damage control. Conversely, a lot of the politicians see the bureaucracy as frustrating, lacking in vision and deeply conservative. They consider the bureaucrats rarely support anything innovative and are often obstructive and running their own agenda.

But the two sides need each other, so they make it work. Their interactions are like theatre. Bureaucrats that rule vast empires with iron fists treat ministers with a deference school teachers can only dream of. In meetings they bow their heads, clasp their hands in their laps and dispense their advice in self-effacing tones. The politicians, and particularly their young staff, shuffle awkwardly in their leather seats at the façade of their superiority. Under the veil of politeness, the two sides play out their struggles. Some days the bureaucrats win, and some days it is the politicians' turn.

How the Public Service works

It is common for people to think of the bureaucracy as a homogeneous monolith. The reality couldn't be further from the truth. Many of government's most important struggles are the tussles between bureaucratic empires. Government is organised into departments dealing with policy areas ranging from foreign affairs to social security, health, transport, industry, the environment and communications. The different departments have their own cultures, agendas and goals. The differences permeate every aspect of how they operate. The delineation is so clear that public servants joke about the cultural stereotypes applied to each department.

The 30-something guy in the thousand-dollar suit, with slick hair and plum private school accent, will be from Foreign Affairs. He will assert the importance of our international obligations and how decisions will be perceived by our trading partners. The 30-something woman dressed in natural fibres, with dangly earrings and wild curly hair, will be from Environment. She'll raise the ecological impacts of a policy and the need for community consultation. The middle-aged guy with the beard and brown cardigan will be from Transport or Primary Industries. He will argue about industry impacts or the consequences for small farming communities. The middle-aged woman in the bright coloured blouse will be from Social Security. She will talk about the need to cushion the impact on communities, but will argue with the Primary Industries officer about special deals not interfering with the rest of the social security payments.

Or that is the stereotype. Nonetheless, the different departments usually identify with the groups they are working for and champion their interests. They wage endless wars against one another trying to get their agenda to the fore.

There is a hierarchy among the departments. The most important delineation is between the 'central co-ordinating' departments and the 'line' departments that have responsibility for a particular policy area. In the federal government, the central departments are the Department of the Prime Minister and Cabinet, the Treasury, and the Department of Finance and Administration. These three control the whole of government agenda and the purse strings. Prime Minister and Cabinet manages the Cabinet – the government's highest decision-making committee – and provides all of the Prime Minister's briefings and policy advice. Treasury is responsible for the broad economic policy settings, like the size of the government deficit. And Finance controls the budget. They decide what gets funding and what doesn't.

These departments are powerful not only because of the jobs they do. Their most important source of power is that they control the information flow to the three most powerful members of the government. They set the agenda for the Prime Minister, the Treasurer and the Minister for Finance. This has a string of consequences.

How economic rationalism infiltrates the decision-making process

Government makes decisions at a number of different levels. Minor administrative decisions are often made by bureaucrats. More important decisions have to be made by the politicians, who are accountable to the electorate. Many of these decisions are made by ministers, the politicians who are responsible for overseeing a department. But the most important decisions are made by Cabinet. The Cabinet is a committee of government ministers that is chaired by the Prime Minister. It is at Cabinet level, the highest level of decision making, that economic rationalism comes to the fore.

Economic rationalism kicks in at the highest level of government decision making because that is when the central co-ordinating agencies are most active. The way the system works is that, when an important decision has to be made, such as a major change to child support payments, a multimillion-dollar rail project or a negotiating position for international greenhouse gas emissions agreements, the issue will go to Cabinet. The minister responsible for the policy area will have his or her department write a 10-page submission. That submission will outline the issue, explain the options and make a recommendation about what the Cabinet should decide. The minister has to circulate the submission several (theoretically 10) days in advance of the Cabinet meeting. This allows the bureaucrats in all the relevant departments to read the submission and to brief their ministers on whether or not to agree with its recommendations.

The first thing the central agency bureaucrats do after reading the submission is to get on the phone to each other. They debate the issues. They usually aim to come up with a shared position, particularly if they dislike what the other department is pushing and want to block it. They often aim to ensure that the Prime Minister, the Treasurer and the Minister for Finance all receive the same advice. The ideal is to have the three most powerful people in the meeting briefed to argue for the same position. This almost guarantees that the central agencies will win the day.

(That is, unless the lobby groups have swung into action, or the issue is splashed across the front page of the newspapers. In which case, the political imperative takes over and the bureaucracy is often ignored.)

The central agencies vet almost all of government's most important decisions. Everything that matters goes through the central agency filter. These agencies are also the heart of economic rationalism – in effect, an economic rationalist filter. Their unique character makes them a breeding ground for economic rationalism.

How central agencies make decisions

The difference between the central agencies and the line departments is not only how much power they have, but also how they make decisions. Their decision-making processes spring from their role in the total government picture.

Government is enormous. A huge number of issues confront government every day. The information management task is vast. It is not possible for one person, or even a single team of hundreds of people, to be across all of the detail of all of the issues confronting a government on any one day. Government's approach to tackling this information problem is to divide up the work between the line agencies and the central agencies. Each line agency knows a lot about a small number of issues. In line agencies each bureaucrat works on an issue or a narrow group of issues. They will know all about the legislation, the personalities, the idiosyncrasies and the history of a particular international agreement, industry start-up program or environmental disaster. By contrast, central agencies have to be across everything. Each central agency bureaucrat will have a broad brushstroke understanding of dozens of issues. But it means they don't know very much about each one. The ideal of this system is that the line agency will provide depth and the central agencies will provide breadth. The line agency can detail the options for a railway contract being negotiated with a state government. And the central agency will know how that contract affects other intergovernmental agreements. Or that is the theory.

Economic rationalism's grip on power comes from the central agency combination of having a powerful filtering role and not knowing very much about each issue. The imperative of time means that the more powerful people become, the more important ideology and values are in their decision making. This quirk arises because of the time it takes for people to absorb information. As people become more powerful they make more and more decisions in a day. As a result, they make their decisions on the basis of less and less information. In the vacuum of detailed information, assumptions fill the gaps. In the absence of evidence to the contrary, people assume that the world works according to their prejudices. Their ideology slips into gear.

This phenomenon underpins decision making in the central agencies. It is common for central agency bureaucrats to have to brief their ministers in very short timeframes. They might have never heard of the issue. But they will have to scramble to do all the research they can, write a brief and clear it through their hierarchy in only a few hours. The short timeframe creates a vacuum of detailed information. The gap in the information is filled by neo-classical economics. They will seek input from the line agency, but they filter all the information they receive through their economics framework. They have a mental checklist they apply to everything that comes across their desks. In the rush, anything that falls outside the framework is discarded. If it doesn't register on the checklist it is ignored. It is this checklist, this framework for thinking about issues, that is the economic rationalist filter.

Economic rationalism's secret weapon

However, economic rationalism's greatest weapon is not its institutional power. Its longevity is not guaranteed by its role in the government decision-making process alone. Its greatest source of power is that its practitioners *believe* in it. It is their conviction that they are on the side of good and righteousness that makes it unshakeable. It is this belief that enables economic rationalists to consistently argue and defend their position when challenged by politicians and other bureaucrats. It enables them to dismiss the public outcry and the endless critiques. It is their confidence that they are doing the right thing that enables them to shrug off the endless barrage of attacks as 'the punters' not understanding the economic wisdom.

Some will argue that if economic rationalists are really well meaning, then surely a certain amount of common sense should prevail. How could a group of highly intelligent people not see the broader issues? How can they ignore concerns that litter the newspapers and are glaringly obvious to the broader community? Paul Krugman, a leading contemporary economist, puts his finger on the problem:

> the strategic omissions in building a model [theory] almost always involve throwing away some real information … and yet once you have a model it is almost impossible to avoid seeing the world in terms of that model – which means focusing on the forces and effects your model can represent and ignoring or giving short shrift to those it cannot. The result is that the very act of modeling has the effect of destroying knowledge as well as creating it. A successful model enhances our vision, but it also creates blindspots.

The central agencies are groups of people that are highly trained in the use of one particular model. They are immersed in it, using it day in, day out, surrounded by people seeing the world through the same lens. They have been trained to analyse problems in a particular way, and have become blind to seeing things any other way. These elite, highly trained bureaucracies systematically overlook a string of issues that a casual observer sees clearly.

This blinkeredness is sustained by their unique position. The central agencies are the most insular decision makers in government. Politicians are deeply immersed in their communities. Most have rigorous schedules of endless community functions, business breakfasts and discussions with their constituencies. Line departments also make an effort to be in touch with their stakeholders. They liaise extensively with the groups affected by their decisions. Major initiatives almost always go out to consultation, where they talk to the wider community and get their input. But central agencies don't. Their officers never leave Canberra's prestigious parliamentary triangle. They never deal directly with the community.

They talk almost entirely to each other. In fact, they joke that if they talked to the community they would risk getting 'captured' and losing their impartiality.

As a result, their model for how the world works is hardly ever tested. They rarely have to deal with people who think differently for an extended period of time. And they are rarely involved in anything in enough detail to see how their models line up with on-the-ground realities over which they are presiding. They maintain a comfortable arm's length from the people and problems over which they have so much power.

Contagion

Economic rationalism's grip on the central agencies means that it spreads to the line departments and the political parties. Line departments know that to get their policies up they must get the central departments on board. They head-hunt ex-central agency bureaucrats and economists to learn how the central agencies think. They have begun to tailor their own policy development and policy proposals around getting through the central agency hoops. Self-censorship has kicked in. Increasingly, they put their proposals through the economic rationalist checklist before even approaching the central agencies.

The politicians also jump onto the economic rationalist bandwagon. While the parties are affected by the current intellectual debate and by their counterparts in the USA and the UK, the bureaucracy set a lot of the terms and language of the policy debate. The bureaucracy is acknowledged as the experts. And the central departments are the elite of the bureaucracy. When all the heavy-weights are imbued with the 'economic wisdom', most up-and-comers conform to the economic framework for fear of being labelled 'soft' or 'not educated enough'. They become groupies of the dominant culture.

Tackling economic rationalism

It is easy to be both too cynical and not cynical enough of politicians and government. When put in a position of saving their own political skins, many politicians do appalling things. They fiddle budget numbers, pay off vested interests, scare-monger and appeal to the lowest common denominator of tabloid headlines. They can be deceptive, dishonest and make decisions they know are not in the community interest. And at times bureaucrats aren't a lot better. However, the bulk of the time the media aren't watching, marginal seats aren't at stake, and their careers aren't on the line. Most of the time, most people in government are trying to make the world a better place. They are making a genuine effort to do what they believe is the right thing. Of course, there are bastards in everything, and there are bastards in politics and government. But there are also a lot of idealistic souls who are there to fight for what they believe in. There is a genuine ethos of public service. Government manifests the struggle between the very best and very worst of human nature. And despite the hype that government is in decline, that struggle is alive and well in our nation's capital.

The challenge of economic rationalism is that it is not about a struggle between the best and worst parts of human nature. It is a genuine debate about how to build a better future. Most of the nation's most powerful economic rationalists are convinced they are on the side of righteousness. Many economic rationalists would describe themselves as being left of centre and as having a deep concern about social issues. They could be found at Aboriginal reconciliation marches. Some are more socially conservative, and quite a substantial number are regular churchgoers. But almost all are convinced that they are setting society on the right path. They believe their prescriptions will build the foundations of a better future.

The task of bridging the divide between the policy experts and the wider community is threefold. First, we have to convince the economic rationalists that their framework is not the 'scientific value-free tool' they like to think it is. We must illuminate that it is based on a worldview and expose its values. Second, we must highlight the blindspots in its worldview. We must pinpoint why its oversights create bad policies and attract the community's ire. And, third, we have to come up with an alternative framework that brings the two sides together. The central agencies of government cannot operate without their checklists. And in the absence of a better one, they will stick with what they've got. We have to provide a new way forward that enables the policy makers and the community to debate the issues on the same terms and to find some common ground.

This task is inherently conceptual. High-level decision making occurs at the level of broad concepts, so if we want to influence it we have to argue at that level. Fortunately this is easier than it sounds. Most people's conflicts with economic rationalism aren't about marginal costs, price elasticities and indifference curves. Economic rationalism is based on a worldview. It has a particular view of what drives people's decisions, how the world works and what the ideal world should be like. When most people attack economic rationalist decrees, it is because they disagree with that worldview. This is a debate we are all equipped to participate in.

Part II

Getting a Handle on Economics

Chapter 4

Is economics a science?

Nothing is more damning than being told you are wrong by a scientific expert. Science has an insurmountable status. It is knowledge. It is truth. It towers above opinion, argument and, above all, ideology. Economics has that scientific status. But it also gets slammed as rampant ideology: a right-wing agenda to drain the world of human values. The casual observer gets caught between the two arguments. Criticisms of economics as a series of abstract models removed from the real world ring true. But so do the scientific credentials. Economists are clever people who have committed their lives to studying this stuff. They must know, right?

Most economic rationalists believe in economics' scientific credentials. They will protest that economics is not an ideology, that it is simply a tool. They will insist it is a value-free body of knowledge that can be used to deliver a wide range of goals. But such assertions reflect a poverty in economics teaching, and they run to the heart of why economic rationalism has been so hard to dislodge. The conviction that economics is a value-free science has been the buffer that has protected economic rationalism from its critics. It has enabled the central agency bureaucrats to cling to their decision-making checklists despite the rising tide of public discontent.

To tackle economic rationalists effectively, we have to recognise that economics is both science and an ideology. Economics is a valid scientific endeavour with noble aspirations. It is also deeply entrenched in ideology. The two are intimately intertwined and all too often become confused.

The job of all sciences (natural and social) is to explain our world. To make sense of what we see around us. But, instead of being seen as 'truth', it should be seen as systematically developed 'convincing stories'. Scientists collect 'facts' and 'observations'. They create theories or stories that explain those facts. The stories change over time. They change as scientists come across new facts and new observations. They change as scientists come up with better and more powerful ways of explaining the facts at hand.

Take the history of astronomy as an example. For centuries, people believed that the earth was flat and that the stars rotated around the earth. When telescopes improved in the Middle Ages, new facts and new observations mounted up. The old theories struggled to explain the new facts, so new theories were created. The new theories tried to keep faith with the old idea that the stars were moving around the earth. But it was not easy. The theories became more and more complicated. They had to include all sorts of exceptions, caveats and truncating theories to be able to explain the new observations. Eventually Copernicus came up with another theory. He argued that the earth rotates around the sun. His new explanation was much simpler than the old ones. With one powerful story he could explain all of the new facts and observations. Eventually his theory became the new scientific orthodoxy, the dominant theory for explaining the facts.

This has been the standard evolutionary path of science. Even the greatest scientific discoveries have been revised and rewritten. Newton's laws of physics were one of the greatest feats in the history of science. They were confirmed by countless successful predictions. But they were later challenged by Einstein's work. They were tinkered with and fine-tuned. The story was changed. It was replaced with one that was more powerful at explaining all the evidence.

Natural sciences versus social sciences

The natural sciences and the social sciences share the goal of explaining the world. But the task is much tougher for the social sciences. It is much tougher to get a single powerful story that everyone agrees on.

The natural sciences study natural phenomena. The classical scientific method is to reduce most problems to simple events, such as combining two chemicals. Natural scientists aim to isolate the experiment from unnecessary things that could influence the outcome.

They might try to hold wind, temperature and the concentration of the chemicals constant so they do not affect the result and do not need to be woven into the explanation. The scientists build clear and simple stories that explain all of the factors that impact on the experiment. It is relatively easy to convince colleagues that their experiments are right. They can do the experiment over and over to test the theory. And they can challenge anyone in the world to test it in their own laboratory.

The social sciences have a much tougher job. It is harder to come up with a story everyone can agree on at any point in time, let alone through history. The difficulty arises because the social sciences cannot isolate the event they are studying. They try to explain things that happen in our societies, but they cannot escape personalities, culture, history, and the whole gamut of circumstances. There are always a huge number of facts that could impact on the event. The endless possible causes or influences make for endless possible explanations.

For example, in the days and weeks after an election, newspapers are packed with different opinions about what happened and why. The analysts draw on the various facts and observations to weave their own explanations. Take the 1999 Victorian election where longstanding Victorian Premier Jeff Kennett was de-throned:

> the main factor was the backlash in the bush … The truth is that many rural vested interests are being disenfranchised because that is what is supposed to happen with competition reform: those who live off subsidies and monopoly rents have to justify them or lose them. The result is that rural voters feel like things are crook and use the gerrymander to take it out on whoever is in power. (Alan Kohler, *Australian Financial Review*)

Or:

> This will go down in history as one of those rare elections where a government's own campaign actually brought it undone. Even in a sophisticated electorate, familiar with the techniques of commercial marketing, voters still draw the line at a political party being sold just like a brand. Kennett's use of such techniques forced voters to confront

the question of political style. To place such a single minded empha-sis on 'Jeff', even to the extent of preventing candidates from talking to the media, created an impression not just of slick, anti-democratic manipulation, but also of unacceptable arrogance. And arrogance, in Australian politics, is still the cardinal sin. (Hugh Mackay, *Age*)

Sometimes they draw other conclusions from the same informa-tion to provide quite different but equally compelling arguments:

Many Victorians woke yesterday with a huge hangover. The govern-ment has suffered a major protest vote against it … the vote reflected a false view that Jeff Kennett had such a commanding lead a protest could be registered without affecting the overall outcome … voter per-ceptions of a Kennett victory were paradoxically enhanced by Kennett's successful campaign. When contrasted to Bracks' relatively low profile and lack of substantial policy alternatives, the perception of a significant Kennett victory was assured. On Saturday night the mythology of a 'fantastic Labor campaign' flowed more plentifully than the champagne, but the reality was quite different. Kennett out-campaigned Bracks. Yet in a perverse consequence, this ultimately compounded the problem. (Petro Georgiou, *Age*)

Finally, the theories can't be tested because the events can't be repeated in identical circumstances. As a result, while any scientific theory is up for debate and revision, social science theories are almost always hotly contestable.

Social sciences and ideology

Ideology is intimately related to the grand theory area of the social sciences. Grand theories are the social sciences' theories of every-thing. They try to explain how society works. They build stories that explain what human beings are like and how society operates. But, like other social science theories, grand theories are completely contestable. And when a little vested interest is added – we make the small step from grand theory into political ideology.

Grand theories try to capture the big-picture dynamics that drive our societies. Marxist theory is perhaps the most famous example. Writing in the 1800s Karl Marx argued that the economy drives society, that our jobs are an important part of who we are and determine our role in the community. He was particularly focused on whether we own the factories and the resources to make things, or whether we have to sell our labour to 'the owners of capital' so that they can make things. He argued that factory hands and unskilled labourers are at the bottom of the heap. They have to sell their labour to others. They do not have much say over what gets made and how things are done. As a result they have little social status. But wealthy factory owners are powerful – socially and economically. They have control of society's resources and drive the agenda of the day. They decide what gets made, what gets built and what community activities get funded. Marx contended that, because the rich control the means of doing things, they control society. They use their power to stay rich and to exploit the people at the bottom. He argued that to make the world a better place we should overhaul how we organise the economy. The bosses–workers divide should be stripped away. Everyone should own everything, and everyone should work. Equality in the economy would create equality in society. It would create a world where no one is oppressed by others.

Or that was the theory, anyway.

Grand theories are one of the toughest areas to get scientific consensus on. It is very difficult to come up with a powerful story that everyone accepts. The theories usually have three elements: a view of what human beings are like, a view of how society works, and a view of an ideal world. This creates a challenge. Which aspects of human nature do you focus on? Which characteristics of society are the most important? Of all the human values, which ones are the most important for an ideal society? There are so many facts and observations to draw on. There are an infinite number of possible stories for how the world works. Many of the theories are compelling. They powerfully explain things we see around us. But different theories come up with vastly different and often contradictory explanations of the world. As a result, they are always up for debate and criticism.

Grand theories take the small step into political ideology when efforts to explain the world are hijacked by vested interests. Competing explanations are used to push political agendas. Lobby groups draw on different stories to convince governments that business tax should go up or down, or that childcare should be free. The Labor and Liberal parties draw on different explanations to decide whether they should support the unions, or provide free health care or free public education. The academic world of trying to explain how the world works has suddenly slipped into the realm of ideological debate. People are expressing political beliefs about how the world is and they are arguing about how it should be.

But, while the difference between ideology and grand theory is vested interest, it is too narrow to think of the vested interest in purely money terms. Sure, some people push an ideological view because they make a dollar out of it. But ideology is most powerful when the vested interest is emotional – when people's own values, and the way they justify their own lives, are tied up with believing the world works in a particular way. Then the commitment to an ideology becomes deeply personal. The depth of conviction can lead people to wilfully ignore facts that challenge their beliefs and to dismiss alternative explanations of the world.

Economics as a science

Economics has always tried to align itself with the natural sciences rather than the 'wishy-washy' social sciences. It attempts to use natural science methodology. It breaks the economy into parts and looks at each in isolation. It develops 'general' theories for each part – so it has a theory of the firm, a theory of the consumer, and so on. And it tries to test the theory against empirical evidence collected from actual social events. It also clings to a mathematical framework, as maths is the traditional language of science.

But studying the economy has all the problems of a social science. There is a range of possible causes of events in the economy. And theories cannot be convincingly tested. The evidence for testing theories is not pure. It cannot be isolated from completely unrelated factors and the tests can rarely be duplicated.

In fact, economics can be seen to be a member of the school of 'grand theories'. Part II will show that it has the structure of a grand theory. It has a view of what human beings are like, it has a theory of how society works and it gives advice on what we should do to make society better. As a grand theory, economics is a science. It is a genuine effort to try to understand how the world works. But like all grand theories it is also contestable. Its analysis is premised on a story about how the world works. If you do not agree with its view of human nature, how society works or the ideal society – it is perfectly reasonable to reject it and to rip into its policy prescriptions.

As a grand theory, however, economics is also only a small step away from ideology. When pundits zealously embrace economics as the path to truth and light (or at least national well-being), they step out of the world of objective scientific endeavour and into the realm of ideology. They personally invest in a worldview. They become committed to its description of how the world works and how it should work. They see the world through a filtered lens and cease to see economics analysis objectively. They become ideologues. They become economic rationalists.

This book will distinguish between economics as a grand theory and economic rationalism as its ideological offshoot. It is important to do this for a couple of reasons. First, economic rationalism is a simplification of a sub-school of economics called neo-classical economics. It is based on the rules of thumb drawn from the neo-classical model of perfect competition. While most of the critiques of economic rationalism can be applied to neo-classical economics, occasionally economic rationalists will push policies that are at odds with a careful application of neo-classical economics. Lipservice is sometimes made to the more sophisticated parts of neo-classical economics in policy circles. But when the pressure is on and meetings need to be wrapped up and press releases written, the simpler broad assumptions about how the world works tend to be what drives decisions.

The second reason for distinguishing between the two is that neo-classical economics is a theory, while economic rationalism has become a worldview. It has become the set of assumptions that central agency bureaucrats make about the world when they pick up any issue. It is no longer a model of the world. It is an ideology.

Conclusion

The conviction that economics is a value-free science has been the bulwark of economic rationalism's power. It has enabled economic rationalists to dismiss their critics as 'not understanding'. The next five chapters aim to achieve a number of goals at once. First, they systematically demonstrate that economic rationalism is a worldview. They expose its view of human nature, its view of how society works and its view of the ideal society. They will prove that it is in essence an ideology that others in the broader community legitimately disagree with. Second, they will pit economic rationalism's worldview against an alternative view that is widely held. I will call it the 'punters' worldview. The aim is to highlight the gulf in values between our most powerful policy makers and the wider community. And, third, it will use the points of conflict between the two views to highlight the holes in the economic rationalist framework and the source of the electorate's disillusionment with government.

Chapter 5

Key ideas in economics

To tackle economic rationalism, we must understand its framework. It is common for critics of economic rationalism to attack economics as being only about money, to argue that economic rationalists do not care about people, quality of life, ethics or values. But, from the economic rationalists' perspective, what they are doing is more noble than most people expect. In their view, they are deeply immersed in the task of trying to improve the lot of the species. They are on a quest to find the best way to improve our material well-being.

Economic rationalism is an offshoot of a school of economic thought called 'neo-classical economics'. I will explain its key ideas and then pinpoint where economic rationalism leaps off. For simplicity I'll refer to neo-classical economics as 'economics'.

Economics immerses itself in the problem of how to use society's resources to deliver the highest possible standard of living. Economics identifies the problem as one of *scarcity*. The problem is that, as a society, we have a finite pot of resources. Those resources are defined as our natural resources, human labour, technology and all of the capital (the buildings, roads, machines and factories) we have already built. The problem of scarcity is how to use these resources to deliver the highest possible standard of living. It is a question of how to employ them to provide the food, shelter, medical services, movies, cars and holidays we want most. This problem is made particularly difficult because we want more material things than our resources could possibly stretch to. In fact, economics assumes our wants are infinite. It argues that no matter how much we have, we will always want more.

The problem of scarcity means that economics is never asking whether a hospital is important enough to be built. It is always asking whether our resources should be used to build that hospital, this school or those roads. It assumes that all our resources are always fully utilised. Everything that we build or make is coming at the cost of building or making something else. Every time we increase funding to one thing, we must cut another. When we pour resources into one industry we are depriving another industry of those same resources. The challenge is to work out how much of our resources we should put into cars, movies and makeovers versus good wine, cheap cigarettes and funky hair ties. It is a question of what combination of goods and services would make society best off.

This is an enormous co-ordination task. It is not just a matter of getting all the basic volumes right. It is then a matter of how we co-ordinate the whole exercise. How do we make sure we have not only the right number of cars, but also the right amount of petrol to run them? How do we decide not only how much breakfast cereal to make, but also how much milk, sugar and how many spoons and bowls we need? The task is enormous and the problem of how to solve it vexing. Or, economists argue, it would be if the market didn't offer the answer.

The grand democracy of consumption

Economics argues that the market naturally and spontaneously solves this problem in most cases. The market creates a grand democracy of consumption. Economics' central argument is that what consumers choose to buy drives what the economy makes and how our resources are used. That what we spend our money on informs and controls the use of our resources. It claims that this process is not only democratic, providing us all with choice and freedom about what we want to consume, but also the most effective way to get the highest possible human welfare out of our finite pot of resources. It is not just quite a good way of doing it, it is the perfect way of doing it.

How the market achieves this awesome task can be explained in three steps. The first is how the consumer behaves, the second is how business behaves, and the third is how the market brings these two together through prices to create the best outcome for all.

Consumer behaviour

The first challenge is to get consumers to reveal what they would really like to have. Economic theory argues that no one knows what goods and services people really want. Only consumers themselves know what they really value and what they desire most. The best way to get people to shed light on what they value is to put them on a tight budget and ask them what they would buy. The argument is that people will be prepared to spend a lot of money on things they value highly, and less on things they don't value as much. Whenever we buy an item at some level, we weigh up the other things we could do with the money and what is worth more to us. The profile of what individuals spend therefore reflects what they really value.

Business behaviour

Economic theory argues that businesses aim to make as much profit as possible. Profit is the difference between how much it costs to make a product and the price it can be sold for. As a result, businesses will leap on any opportunity where the price is high and the costs of production are low. Businesses' drive to make a profit means that they will push into the most profitable markets first, where their products are highly valued but don't use many resources. Once all the high-profit opportunities have been taken up, businesses will move into slightly less profitable industries where the price is still higher than the cost of making the goods, but the gap is not as big. Last of all, businesses will go into industries where the price only just covers the cost of making a good. Of course, they will never get into making goods which cost more to make than people are prepared to pay, because they would make a loss. In this way, businesses' pursuit of profit systematically targets society's resources at making the things consumers value most, focusing on the ones that use the least resources first, and then moving on to goods that either take more resources to make or are not as highly valued.

The price mechanism

The market brings together consumers and businesses. It co-ordinates them through the market price. If consumers value a product highly and are prepared to pay a high price for it, then the high price will encourage business to make a lot of the product. However, if consumers don't value the product very highly and are only prepared to pay a low price for it, businesses will make a smaller amount of the product.

The process of consumers making sure they get the best value for money out of their budget will make sure that society gets the best value for money out of its resources. If a product becomes too expensive, consumers will decide they will get better value from buying something else. When they shift their spending from one product to another, they shift resources from one sector of the economy to another. If lots of people go from buying sneakers to buying takeaway food, shoe shops will close and more takeaway places will open. Some people in the shoe industry will lose their jobs, but new jobs will open up in takeaway food. The use of resources will reflect what people get the most pleasure from, given the cost of making them.

The importance of competition

Competition in the market is vital to get the best use of resources. It is vital because it prevents businesses from pocketing all of the profit. The theory is that businesses compete against each other. First, to woo customers away from their competitors, they compete to provide the products and the service people want most. They tailor their products to our specific wants. Second, they compete by undercutting their competitors' prices. The theory is that businesses will keep trying to undercut each other's prices to win customers. The benefit of this competition is that it squeezes the businesses' profit margin. The business will cut costs by using resources in the most efficient way they can, so as to improve their profit margin. But, eventually, even that will be eroded by competition. In the long run, business will have no choice but to set its price as near as dammit to what the product costs to make.

Eventually, economics argues that market prices will reflect the relative costs of making products. The prices of jeans, sneakers, cars and eggbeaters reflect the relative amounts of resources that are needed to make them. Anywhere that there is a gap between the price and the cost of making a product, entrepreneurs will step in. If an industry is making big profits, entrepreneurs will pull their money out of low-performing activities and put it into high-performing activities. They will leap into action and go into the market. Thus, by increasing the supply of hair sprays or gloss lipsticks, they introduce more competition. This will eventually bring prices down and they will end up with prices that more or less equal the cost of making the product.

The way it all comes together

Economic theory argues that this process acts to target resources at the things we want most. Initially businesses concentrate on providing the cars, clothes and CDs we want most and that are cheapest to make. The process of competition erodes business profit margins so that the relative prices of goods eventually reflect the relative cost of making them. By means of the price, consumers are able to line up how much they value different products with the cost to our resources of making them. This is the crucial condition for making sure the market delivers the best possible mix of goods and services. This enables the shopper to pick the combination of products that gives them the greatest satisfaction for the least resources.

Economic theory argues that this 'grand democracy of consumption' is not just a good way to solve 'the problem of scarcity', it is the best way. If consumers act perfectly rationally and businesses act perfectly rationally and everyone is perfectly informed, this process is mathematically optimal. It could not be done better.

There are five rules of thumb that economic rationalists take from this:

- The problem they are trying to solve is the allocation of scarce resources.
- The market targets our resources at making the goods and services we value most.
- The price of a particular good determines how much of it is made.

- In the end, there will be similar profit levels across different sectors of the economy.
- Government should not distort the market. We should let the market operate freely to create maximum wealth, and then redistribute the wealth afterwards to achieve any social goals.

This is the point at which economic rationalism and economic theory part ways. Economic theory investigates these broad principles in more detail. Economic theorists apply these principles to different markets, products and institutional settings. They make all sorts of caveats and exceptions about how these principles can be applied and what the consequences might be. But economic rationalists charge forth and apply these principles with impunity. They use them as their rule of thumb for understanding the world. Central agency bureaucrats apply them to every issue that comes across their desks. They permeate the assumptions of almost all of the policy advice given to the Prime Minister, the Treasurer and the Minister for Finance.

Some familiar applications of economic rationalism

Price controls

Economic rationalists often argue that governments should not intervene in markets and mess around with prices. The theory behind their argument is that the price determines how much of a product gets made. Government interference in prices will result in the wrong amount of the product being made, our resources being misused and the total welfare of the community being eroded.

For example, take rent controls. At different times it has been suggested that governments should legislate to put a ceiling on rent prices. Economic theory argues that a law to keep rent prices below the market price will create a housing shortage. First, entrepreneurs will shift their money into other sorts of investment because the rental property market will be less profitable. Other second-choice investments will become more attractive and the investment dollars will flow out of the rental market. The drop in price will spark a cut-back in available accommodation.

Second, at the same time the number of people seeking rental property will increase. People who would otherwise have kept living at home or in share houses will decide that, at the lower price, rental accommodation is good value for money. The outcome will be a housing shortage. There will be more people wanting rental properties than are available. In this way, economic theory argues, government's attempts to improve the market would actually reduce the welfare of society.

Protection

Governments are often called upon to protect industries through tariffs, quotas or regulations. Economic rationalists argue that this sort of interference in the market also reduces the welfare of the community, by mucking up the market's ability to target resources at where they are most valued.

Take the example of tariffs. If the government puts a 20% tariff on computers being imported, a business importing a $1000 one will have to pay $200 in tax, pushing the price of the computer up to $1200. The jump in the price of imported computers might be enough to make Australian computer manufacturing viable. They might be able to compete if the market price was $1200, but would not be profitable if the price was only $1000. However, according to economic rationalists, this is a bad thing.

They argue that it is a problem for three reasons. First, a lot of people who would have bought a computer for $1000 won't get the benefit of owning one because of the higher price. Second, those who do buy are paying an extra $200 for their computers. It is a $200 that they would otherwise have spent on something else, keeping other industries in business. And, third, a lot of businesses use computers. The increase in computer price boosts their business costs. By adding the $200/computer to their bottom-lines, they become relatively less profitable and the goods they make relatively more expensive. As a result, economic rationalists argue that the policy benefits the small local industry, but inflicts costs on a whole range of others. They insist the net effect is negative for society.

Economic rationalists argue that the tariffs should be slashed. The computer industry should be allowed to collapse for the benefit of consumers, sectors of the economy that would otherwise get the $200, and businesses that rely on computers. They argue that the resources invested in the computer manufacturing industry should be shifted into something more profitable, something that would make a bigger contribution to the welfare of the community. The labour should move into a different industry. And the money invested in the factories should be freed up to be put into more profitable activities, ones that will make a greater net contribution to society.

Free trade

The free trade argument is in part a tariff argument. But it is also a scarce resources argument. It is an argument that, if we only have a finite set of resources, we should specialise in doing the things we do best. That, if another country can make undies more cheaply than we can, it is in our best interests to buy our undies from them. Instead of tying up our resources, we should shift our resources into industries we can do more cost effectively than anyone else can. The idea is that, if we specialise in what we are best at, we will be better off. We will make bigger profits by exporting what we are good at and buying imported undies with the proceeds. The result, the economic rationalists insist, is a net gain for society.

In fact, economic rationalists argue, if other countries want to subsidise their undies industry to undercut our industry, that is just fine. We should take the extra cheap undies and say 'thanks very much'. They argue that there are benefits for Australia in getting into the free trade/specialising in the things we are best at game, even if no one else will play. Shifting our resources out of industries other countries do more cheaply is an advantage to us. We can take the cost advantage of buying it cheaply from them, and then put our own resources to better use.

You will notice that this way of analysing problems assumes full employment and that resources can be shifted from one industry to another relatively easily. Economic rationalists acknowledge this process isn't as easy as all that. However, they argue that their policies lead to short-term pain for vocal minorities but have greater long-term benefits for the wider society.

An important aside

As you may have noticed, this theory does not address economic growth. Most economic growth comes from an expansion of our pot of resources – technology, capital (factories, machinery, infrastructure), labour – and our use of our natural resources. That economic theory focuses on the problem of scarcity reflects that it was developed by philosophers and bureaucrats trying to work out how to organise society rather than by businesspeople trying to work out how to make money. The area of economics that economic rationalists draw their rules of thumb from is called 'allocative statics'. It makes up the core of first and second year microeconomics in most universities. It is called statics because it is about how to solve a problem in a single timeframe where you have a finite pot of resources that isn't changing, and allocative because the problem you are trying to solve is how to allocate those resources.

Economic rationalists generally assert that competition will push businesses to find better ways of doing things and new ways to make money, and that this will drive growth. Despite the regularity with which you hear this assertion, it is not a very well developed part of economic theory. Of the work done in the last 10 years, the bulk supports or assumes that view. However, a minority of work has explored the ways in which competition can inhibit growth. Competition can undermine optimal investment in technology, corporate secrecy can mean that new and better ways of doing things are slow to spread, and corporate strategies can mean businesses spend more time working out how to nobble each other than how to push ahead. Nonetheless, the massive growth of market economies over the last century does imply that competition and growth get along pretty well most of the time.

However, it is important to recognise that most of the debate on freeing up markets is not about growth, as you would tend to expect. It's mainly about efficiency in allocative statics.

Conclusion

I hope that at this point you are finding economic rationalism more compelling and interesting than you had expected. It is a powerful set of ideas. It is not surprising that a lot of people are swept up in its explanatory insight and in the order and simplicity it brings to a complex world. But, before you become a born-again economic rationalist, take a step back. There are good reasons why politicians spouting economic wisdom make the pit of your stomach uneasy. There is a legitimate basis to that niggling concern that what they are saying isn't quite right. To put our finger on exactly why, we have to draw out economic rationalism's worldview.

Part III

Revealing Economic Rationalism's Worldview

Chapter 6

'Punters' versus 'economic rationalists'

Economic rationalism is based on a worldview. That worldview is steeped in values. The values flow from both the ideas it asserts and the issues it ignores. It is economic rationalism's blind spots, the things it deems irrelevant to how the world works, that are the greatest points of conflict. By peeling back the layers of economic analysis we reveal this worldview and shine some light into its darker crevices.

There are three parts to economic rationalism's worldview to investigate: its view of human nature, its view of how society works, and its view of the ideal society. These parts are bound by an internal logic. Human nature drives how society works. The ideal is based on delivering the things that matter most to people and on harnessing society's resources to do it. Together the three parts are a conceptually coherent map to human society.

The sharp edges and blind spots in this worldview can be highlighted by pitting it against a conflicting view. I have constructed one that I believe is widely held in Australia. For the purpose of being inflammatory, I'll call it 'the punters' worldview'. I won't attribute it to anyone in particular. Political theory buffs will notice it comes from the 'social' end of the political spectrum. In American politics it would count as left of centre without being socialist or communist. In Australia it is powerful because it can be used to explain some of the ideas of groups as diverse as One Nation, the Greens, the Democrats, the union movement, and various parts of the divided left.

A warning to the uninitiated – the worldviews sketched out below are to the real world as stick figures are to a portrait. They are bold straight lines. Portraits are fleshy, complex and the lines are almost always fuzzy. They starkly present ideas and themes that we only notice operating subtly at the level of subtext and assumption. They can run the risk of overstating the case and should be treated carefully. People may hold these worldviews (or part of them) as one of many ideas and beliefs. Care should be taken in attributing them to anyone. But they are powerful tools for understanding these debates.

Chapter 7

Contrasting views of human nature

Generally, we do not think too much about what it is to be human. What we are like, the point of our lives – except in our sombre moments – slips by like a shadow in the darkness. The issues are only thrown into focus when we hit a different view. Usually it is a conflict of values with someone we know intimately. The partner who only cares about the tidy house, the big promotion and whether the car is a recent model. Or the one who is not ambitious enough, gives too much to charity or spends too much time in the garden. In a moment of clarity we know s/he is not seeing the world the way we do. We are incredulous that they can be so oblivious to reality. These are the worst fights. At their core they are conflicts about human nature and how the world is.

The split between economic rationalists and the wider community sometimes has echoes of those fights with a lover. There is that same sense of exasperation, that those in power are not seeing the world the same way as the rest of the community. As the economic rationalist spiel flies past, it is hard to pinpoint exactly what we are disagreeing about, let alone convince the other side of our view.

The economic rationalists' view

Just as our own outlook on the world is built on ideas about human nature, so are intellectual theories of society. Economic rationalists' picture of human nature is the basis of the conflict between the policy elite and the wider community. Most of the spats stem in part or entirely from this conflict. But it is not a question of whether people are greedy and self-interested or not. The conflict is more subtle than that.

Like other theories of society, economic rationalism has a view of human nature, but it is buried in its models. To find it we need to dig around. This view can be split into two parts. First, how people relate to each other and fit together to make up society. And, second, what drives us to do the things we do.

How society fits together

Economic rationalists' assumptions about human nature wash past unnoticed when the theory is first explained. They are initially elusive because they are built into the way economic rationalists look at a problem. When they analyse the economy they break it down into its parts and look at each bit separately.

For example, when they look at the clothing market, they divide it into people buying clothes and businesses selling clothes. Then they break it down further. Instead of looking at all clothes shoppers they look at a single clothes shopper. And instead of looking at all clothing businesses they look at a single clothing business. To build their model of the market, economic rationalists model what one (imaginary) clothes shopper would do to rationally pursue his or her self-interest. They then apply that single shopper's behaviour to all clothing shoppers. They say that all one hundred, or one million or ten million, clothes shoppers would behave identically to the one shopper they modelled. They do the same with clothing businesses. They model what one (imaginary) business would do to make the biggest possible profits. They then apply the same behaviour to all clothing businesses.

Bang! The level playing field is born. This approach assumes we are all identical. When it applies the model of one person to all people, it assumes we are all faced with the same decisions and make them in the same way. We all have the same opportunities, the same skills and the same interests.

Economic rationalists do believe that people want different things. They agree that teenage girls are likely to spend more on clothes, pensioners are likely to spend more on health care and that wealthy businesspeople are more likely to employ tax lawyers. However, economic rationalists do not consider these differences important in understanding how the economy works. They argue that what people want is their affair and that private preferences are none of their concern. All that matters is that the economy deliver what people are seeking. As a result, economic models do not distinguish between these groups of people. They do not consider them to have different roles in the economy, or to be pursuing different things or facing different obstacles. In economic models, people are equal individuals pursuing whatever consumption they desire.

What drives people

The next question is: what do economic rationalists assume drives our behaviour? The catchcry we hear is that the rational pursuit of self-interest is the key. We have heard it so often we take it for granted. It seems self-evident. But this broad sweeping statement is a shield. It protects economic rationalists from scrutiny. It is hard to argue that people act against their own interests. It is even harder to argue that they are not rational. It is only when we look at what economic rationalists mean by self-interest that we realise we are talking about something much more specific. And something much harder to defend.

John Stuart Mill attacked the idea of 'self-interest' when it was first being used over a hundred years ago – and the criticism still stands:

> When we see a man's actions, we know with certainty what he thinks his interest to be. But it is impossible to reason with certainty from what we take to be his interest in his actions. One man goes without a dinner, that he may add a shilling to a hundred thousand pounds; another runs in debt to give balls and masquerades. One man cuts his father's throat to get possession of his old clothes; another hazards his life to save that of an enemy. One man volunteers on a forlorn hope; another is drummed out of a regiment for cowardice. Each of these men has, no doubt, acted from self interest. But we gain nothing by knowing this, except the pleasure, if it be one, of multiplying useless words … it is idle to attribute any importance to a proposition which, when interpreted, means only that a man had rather do what he rather do.

Mills' argument is that there is no generic self-interest. People are driven by their goals, whatever they may be. Self-interest is anything that furthers those goals. When economic rationalism claims that delaying purchases or pushing for higher wages is in our self-interest, it is making assumptions about our goals.

Political economist Robert Reich found that 'rational behavior' hits the same problem. The best way of achieving a goal depends on the situation, which can change if circumstances change. If your goal is to get to work as quickly as possible, and the car is quicker than the train, the rational approach is to take the car. But if there are roadworks on the freeway, the train might be a better option or perhaps even a bike. As a result, there is not a generic 'rational' way of pursing a goal; there is only a best way of doing things under specific conditions.

Economic rationalists model people chasing specific goals bound by specific constraints. This is crucial. If economic rationalism is wrong about people's goals and constraints, its arguments about how people act will be wrong. Take, as an example, the 1998 federal government policy of literacy testing people who apply for unemployment benefits. If they are illiterate they have to attend classes to get their full dole. The government argues that if people have a dollar incentive they will go to classes, improve their literacy and become more employable. It assumes that the only goal for each individual is to have more money and that there are no constraints.

An alternative argument is that the highest priority goal for one illiterate 20-year-old guy is short-term emotional self-preservation. His constraints are that he believes he is stupid and he will never learn to read and write. He also believes he will always be poor. He hates government and figures of authority because of being humiliated in the past. For this bloke the rational course of action is to drop out of the social security system and rely on more dubious sources of income. He avoids the pointless humiliation. Emotionally it is the safer path for right now. By failing to recognise his real goals and real constraints, the policy does not help him to escape the ranks of the long-term unemployed. Instead, it pushes him even further into a social underclass.

The 'rational pursuit of self-interest'

In theory, economic rationalists say that our goal is quality of life, that people are trying to maximise their 'utility' or their personal satisfaction. This means having the combination of things that gives them the highest level of personal enjoyment. It does not have to be material things. It can include enjoying a bushwalk through pristine forests or knowing that your eggs were produced by free-range chooks. However, when policy makers apply models it is not enough to say that people will do whatever makes them feel good. They must tie down what people will actually do. Once the theory is applied to a practical case, 'utility' almost always becomes 'material goods'. As a result they make assumptions about people's goals. They almost always assume that people will go for material things.

Economic rationalists also only set people two constraints in chasing this goal: their budget, and the price of the things they want to buy. There are lots of constraints that might impact on people that economic rationalists don't include. Two of the most important ones are about information and need. But we will come back to them in the next chapter.

The combination of assumptions that we are all identical and the narrow definition of our goals and constraints enables economic rationalists to make broad generalisations about society. These generalisations are made without any reference to their impacts on particular individuals or groups, or how they might affect groups differently: 'When wages fall, businesses will employ more people.' 'When the prices rise, demand will drop.' 'If opened up to competition, businesses will become more efficient.'

Economic rationalists' worldview assumes these 'economic' behaviours go to the core of human nature. In the same way that they apply these behaviours across social groups, they happily apply them to different countries. They assume that, despite cultural differences, economic behaviour runs deep. That people are fundamentally the same across the world, throughout time. That economic behaviour is innate.

The punters' view

He is an old sugarcane grower from Queensland.

She is a 19-year-old greenie activist from the university.

He is a first-generation Asian immigrant studying accounting.

She is a baby-boomer Catholic feminist.

He is an old digger who lived up Bendigo way before going to the war.

These descriptions say nothing about a person's character, but we use them all the time. They are social group labels. How old you are, where you come from, what you do for a job. We use them to describe friends and strangers. We believe they tell us something about a person. That our social groups are part of who we are. They shape our ideas, our values and how we deal with things.

At the core of these beliefs is the assumption that part of our character is born and the other part is socialised. Our communities and our cultures make up part of us. What we learn from our families and others around us shape our skills, our values and our perspective on the world. It often dramatically changes our approach to situations. For example, take this excerpt from *Prisoners of the Japanese* by Gavan Daws. It talks about how, even on the edge of death, World War II prisoners retained powerful cultural identities. Their national characters remained distinct and shaped how they behaved:

> I started coming across national differences in behavior from the very first days of my research, and the evidence kept piling up ... The juices crushed out of the POWs were of course human in the most fundamental sense. But at the same time, all the way down to starvation rations, to a hundred pounds of body weight and less, to the extremities of degradation – all the way to death – the prisoners of the Japanese remained inextinguishably American, Australian, British, Dutch ... The Americans were the great individualists of the camps, the capitalists, the cowboys, the gangsters. The British hung on to their class structure like bulldogs, for grim death. The Australians kept trying to construct little male-bonded welfare states ...

Daws' observation rejects the idea that culture is like clothing covering our true natures. It rejects that in dire circumstances culture is shed to reveal a fundamental human nature. Instead, Daws argues that culture is as integral as our skeletons. It drives how we see the world, how we relate to each other, how we operate and what we value.

How social groups are defined is complicated, and becoming more so. Traditionally groups revolved around religion, locality, profession, income and age. In the past there were fewer and relatively more homogeneous groups. But these days, as society becomes more complex, groups are fragmenting. There are more with their own variants of values, opportunities and constraints. Also, most of us can be lumped into a number of different groups at any one time. We draw our values from various influences. A young country woman may share some values with young women in the cities. But at the same time she might believe in her grandfather's religion and take her economic ideas from her regional community. Each of us is a hybrid, taking different bits from all the groups we belong to. Nonetheless, in this increasingly complicated world, these groups remain one of the most important means by which we try to understand how our communities work.

What drives us

In the punters' view, our goals come from our communities. We all want to be seen as successful. We want our parents to be proud of us, to respect us and value us. As kids we learn what counts as good in our community. We learn what a successful person is. Whether it is having money, power, or professional success, or being good looking, a good footy player, generous and funny, or just a good bloke. We spend our lives wanting to be these things. We set out to make a million dollars, win the Nobel Prize or make it as a professional footballer.

In a business sense this translates into people in different groups having different goals. A person from one social group might want the security and status of pulling a six-figure salary. But kids from another group will never consider that a possibility. They will stick to the solid reliable trades of their parents. Others again will choose to hang on by a thread if they can run their own business or work on the art, the antiques or the cars that they love. Others will go into public life, politics or running the town pub, putting community identity above the bottom-line. These ideas about a successful life run in social groups.

These social groups are, of course, not completely deterministic. The values we learn from our groups overlay our individual personalities (as well as our talents and capacities). We can throw them off, but it is difficult. Running smack up against our family values can create turmoil, both with our families and within ourselves. It is hard to be looked down on and ridiculed by the people we love. And it is even harder not to loathe ourselves if we take paths we were raised to think are bad or unworthy. Some people do make the break, but most of us stick close to home.

What constrains us

In the social view, our constraints also come from our social groups. Practical barriers like money are part of the picture. But skills and ideas about what is possible are powerful at slamming doors too.

The practical barriers are the ones we hear about most. Access to resources is the key. Money is the obvious one. Whether or not you can get the capital to start a business or buy out a company. Lack of cash or access to credit and assets to underwrite a loan stop many opportunities dead. Access to crucial market information or to a network of customers can also be vital. Getting good deals from wholesalers is essential in competing with established market players. These barriers often come from our social groups. Obtaining risk capital depends on whether your family has the money or whether you can get someone to underwrite a loan. Access to information and networks also depends on our social groups.

Barriers created by skills are also often overlooked, but are just as powerful. Technical skills are obviously important. But lack of skill in getting bank loans, planning permits and government grants can put dreams out of reach. Knowing how things are done, who to approach and how to argue your case are skills we pick up from our families and social groups. Not having them often blocks the way forward. For example, when tackling government a solid knowledge of the selection processes is vital. Applications need to be made in a particular way. Language and tone are important. Knowing the bureaucrats' selection criteria is crucial, as decisions centre on issues the average businessperson does not think of. Knowing who is powerful, who has control of the decisions, how to lobby them and what is appropriate pressure to bring to bear are all a matter of insider knowledge. Some groups are very politically organised and well connected. They play the games much more effectively. Others languish on the outside, not even sure why they are failing.

The most difficult constraint of all is ideas about what is possible. Few people strive for things outside the bounds of their experience. We might dream of them. But we rarely turn abstract ideas into practical steps without reassurance it can be done. Most of us need to know someone who has trodden the path before us, someone we can identify with. The academic world is intimidating to people who have never known a professor or had a friend struggle through a PhD. The fashion industry is mortifying if you have not grown up in those circles. And if the only entrepreneurs you know run the local milkbar, the idea that you could set up a multimillion-dollar business exporting to Asia is remote. Large numbers of us cling to what we know, treading the familiar path of other members in our social groups. Theoretically, a range of economic opportunities is open to all of us. But only a few of us will see them as real options.

Suddenly, in contrast to economic rationalists' view of 19 million people chasing the same goals under the same constraints, we have a different picture. An Australia made up of lots of different social groups, with each group following its own pattern of rational behaviour. Each has a unique path of 'rational self-interest'.

Contrasting the views

Debate between the two views heats up when an issue like university fees hits the agenda. Understanding the two views lifts the lid on the rhetoric we hear so often. The economic rationalist approach is that price is the best way of targeting resources to where they are valued most. They argue that lots of people go to university who wouldn't if they had to foot the bill. That being prepared to pay the cost is a better indicator than entry scores of how much a student wants higher education. As a result, the view is that 'user pays' will bring about the best use of community resources.

This was the thinking when the Howard government hiked up university fees in 1996. The then Minister for Education, Senator

Amanda Vanstone, said the fees would encourage 'poorly moti-
vated medical and law students to make alternative choices'. She
also supported the idea that price was a better discriminator than
talent: 'There'll be a lot of students who are quite bright, they might
get middle 90s, low 90s and they really, really want to do law or
medicine and they're happy to pay to get into the course of their
choice at the university of their choice'.

The punters' view rejects the economic perspective. It argues
that mark-based entry is skewed in favour of kids who are inten-
sively coached through private schools. But that this is still prefer-
able to user pays for three reasons. First, it attacks the level playing
field assumption. It reels at the claim that preparedness to pay
reflects how much people want an education, because it assumes
equal access to money. It assumes that $5000 is the same barrier to
everyone. Wealthy parents often spend in excess of $10,000 a year
in fees to put their children through private schools. Many of them
would not even blink at paying $5000 for university fees. Their kids
may have very little interest in their course of study and still expect
to stroll into law or medicine under user pays. But other students
may have a desperate desire to do law or medicine, and no chance
of being able to get the money together. Their parents may be
unable or unwilling to help, and at 17 or 18 years of age those school
leavers are unlikely to be able to access the money.

The punters' view also argues that deferring the debt is a much
bigger barrier for kids from low-income backgrounds. Different
groups weigh the risk of a $25,000 debt differently. Kids who have
highly paid doctors and lawyers among their family and friends
barely question the investment. They do not see it as a big risk. But
kids who do not know anyone who has successfully become a doctor
or lawyer perceive the risk to be much greater. They are taking the
punt that in 10 years they are going to be earning more money than
anyone they know. This risk is compounded because not every graduate makes a lot of money. And family networks play a role in deter-
mining who becomes a wealthy graduate and who does not.

Another argument from the punters' view is that fees compound
the different cost-benefit analysis already facing poorer kids when
deciding whether to go to university. For them, working to support
themselves cuts into study time. Dealing with family problems and

responsibilities can hit kids from disadvantaged backgrounds harder and more often. Commuting and transport can also be a problem. Campuses are often in wealthy areas. The cheap transport options take time, again cutting into study time, and commuting long distances to university can burst the budget. Kids from low-income backgrounds are also hit by isolation when they go to university, as few of their friends go with them. They find themselves alienated from people they left behind, as family and friends often withdraw their emotional support. They can also lose confidence, suddenly finding themselves surrounded by wealthier kids with better clothes and different life experiences and who have been better prepared by their schools for the university environment.

As a result, when poorer kids are weighing up the costs and benefits of going to university, a lot of things come into their equations that do not impact on better-off kids. Their path of rational self-interest can lead them away from further study. In a society that values education as the escalator to high-paid and high-status occupations, these young people are being systematically marginalised.

Conclusion

Economic rationalists see everyone as being the same, facing the same set of options when they make 'rational self-interested decisions'. This might seem philosophical but it runs to the heart of the conflict between economic rationalists and the rest of the community. The divide translates into a question of whether people should be treated differently. The wider community is more likely to recognise individual circumstances and to believe they should be taken into account. There is a notion that some people are more vulnerable than others and that they should be given a hand up. As a result, the community is more likely to believe that government should cushion the policy impacts on those worst hit.

But economic rationalists do not see it that way. In government departments, the bureaucrats will be conscious of the political sensitivity of an issue. They will brief the Prime Minister if a particular group is going to get rolled and is likely to kick up a fuss and get the issue all over the newspapers. But sweeteners to hard-hit groups are seen to be bad policy. The bureaucrats are focused on the rule of thumb that the unfettered market will deliver the best allocation of resources, that the same market rules should apply to everyone. This or that interest group should not get special treatment. They are convinced they are defending the interests of the taxpayer and the wider community. Support packages are considered to distort the market, to be inefficient and unfair on the rest of the community. They are political compromises that politically astute bureaucrats just have to live with.

Chapter 8

Contrasting views of how society works

'God is dead', the great German philosopher Nietzsche declared at the end of the 19th century, sparking one of the great philosophical debates of the 20th century. He argued that we have to accept that human beings are alone in the world. We have to create the meaning and purpose in our own lives. And we are solely responsible for how our lives go. What has this got to do with economics, you ask? You might be surprised to find you have a position on one of the great debates of last century. You might be even more surprised that this debate creates a rift between economic rationalists and the wider community. The debate strikes at the core of our most fundamental ideas about how the world works.

The economic rationalists' view

Economic rationalism's view of human nature paints a picture of 19 million individuals trotting about Australia greedily chasing their own self-interest. They ruthlessly pursue the almighty dollar with little interaction or consideration of others. But this looks like chaos. How is it tamed into a cohesive society? How can economists model this chaos and say that 'society works like this' generation after generation? The answer, they argue, lies in the underlying logic of the universe.

In the economic rationalist view, natural laws guide the market to harmony. The idea comes from the 18th century Enlightenment scientists' picture of the natural world. They believed that the natural world was a great machine designed by God. They believed that natural laws governed the universe. Left to their own devices, these laws guided the universe to a divine harmony. In 1776 the famous economist Adam Smith first popularised the idea of the 'invisible hand' by applying the same thinking to humans. Based on Smith's work, economics came to argue that there are fundamental laws of the market, that people chasing their self-interest are bound by market forces. The 'invisible hand' would harness people's self-interested behaviour and channel their actions into creating wealth for society. It argues that if people are left to act 'naturally' they slip into feeding this harmonious order. They unwittingly target resources where they are valued most, bringing about the greatest good for society. Our selfish desires drive the wheels of the great natural machine, creating a greater good.

Not convinced? Think about the political mantra of the last two decades – 'unleashing market forces', 'freeing up the market', and the great social benefits of competition. It invokes images of underlying natural forces that need to be freed. It implies there is a natural order lying dormant under layers of government regulation. The rhetoric argues that, if we release the forces of competition, market forces will propel us to wealth and prosperity. In the economic rationalist view these natural forces harness the power of people working against each other for their own gain. It argues that the market uses this negative power to create a greater good.

In this view, the all-powerful market makes government redundant. Pure economic rationalists (in contrast to a range of other economists) argue that government disrupts the natural order. According to this view, most markets work as long as they are not corrupted. Regulations 'distort' markets and throw them into chaos and inefficiency. They distort the price mechanism. They squander resources and discriminate against people. Economic rationalists believe government intervention feathers the nests of the few at the cost of the many.

For example, in economic rationalism's view, car tariffs give one group a profit at the cost of others. By putting a tariff on imported cars, the government pushes up the selling price of cars in Australia. If the government puts a 20% import tariff on a $10,000 car coming from Japan, it will sell in Australia for up to $12,000. This increases the price that Australian manufacturers can sell their cars for. The propped-up price boosts the domestic car industry's profits and guarantees its employees jobs. But the industry's profits are paid for by car buyers, because they pay up to $2000 extra for their new car. The government has guaranteed one group profits at the cost of others. Distorting the market is almost always a disservice to society as a whole, economic rationalists insist. Take this diplomatic statement made by advocates of the National Competition Policy:

> There may be situations where competition, although consistent with efficiency objectives and in the interests of the community as a whole, is regarded as inconsistent with some other social objective. For example, governments may wish to confer special benefits on a particular group for equity or other reasons ... However, it is possible for governments to achieve objectives of these kinds in ways that are less injurious to competition and the welfare of the community as a whole. (*National Competition Policy: Report by the Independent Committee of Inquiry*, August 1993)

Or, again, in 1999:

> National Competition Policy reform often involves removing anti-competitive arrangements that traditionally conferred unfair privileges on sheltered groups – often high income earners – which the rest of the community do not enjoy. (*National Competition Policy: Some impacts on society and the economy*, January 1999)

Economic analysis finds that the market does fail sometimes, creating its own inefficiency and injustice. According to one National Competition Policy report, 'there are some situations where unfettered competition is not consistent with economic efficiency'. However, economic rationalists believe governments often cannot fix the problems. They argue that governments are made up of self-interested people. Politicians only care about what is politically saleable, and bureaucrats strive to build their personal empires. As a result, government is more likely to fail than the market. Human attempts to intervene in the natural order are likely to make things worse rather than better. Governments should just stay out of it, they argue.

This view of the role for government is intertwined and mutually reinforcing of economic rationalism's view of human nature.

In this view, in the absence of government-driven distortions, everyone is equal and has the same opportunities. In the perfectly competitive market, each person and each business is too small a player to manipulate the market. For example, when you go to buy a car you can't convince the dealer to sell it to you for less than market price. There are plenty of other people the dealer could sell the car to. But the dealer also can't ask you to pay more than market price either. You could buy the same car from another dealer. As a result, in economic rationalism's view, neither person can be manipulated by the other. We are free from each other, but are equally contained and constrained by the market.

The same self-reinforcing logic is evident when we look at the social/cultural element in this worldview. In the words of that famous economic rationalist, Baroness Thatcher, 'there is no such thing as society'. In this hard-line view, politics and culture do not rate a mention. Some economic rationalists take a softer line. They argue that the economic system can be separated out from cultural, social and political issues. The economy can be looked at in isolation from these things. In fact, a rule of thumb often taught to young economists is to organise the economy in the most efficient way to make as much wealth as possible and then to divvy up the booty according to political and social values afterwards. Either way, it means that social and cultural issues are not on the map in economic rationalism's view of how society works.

The punters' view

The punters' view is that there is no natural order – or, in Nietzsche's words, God is dead. People cannot rely on natural forces to guide them. We are the authors of our own societies. We have to decide what we want and make it happen. In this view people have to come together and collectively manage themselves. We each take on different roles in the community. The community forms groups and social institutions based largely on roles, whether they are formal industry peak bodies, churches and unions, or gangs of teenage skateboarders. In this view, the task of managing ourselves is complex. We have to manage the competing interests of these often conflicting groups and balance their views about how society should be. In this view, we should manage ourselves through politics and government.

These social groups/institutions can be seen to have a life of their own. We can track the role of the church, the union movement, farmers, Aboriginal communities and the mining industry through history. They evolve and change over the years, sometimes disbanding and new groups forming, but mostly remaining in place for the next generation to move through. The groups are just a collection of individuals, with perhaps a few buildings to house them. What holds them together is that as each generation moves through it learns the ideas and values of the group/institution. Each new generation takes on the mantle of its group's role in society. And it plays out that role as fiercely as generations that have gone before.

In this view, social groups have different roles in society: complementing, constraining and impeding each other. Manufacturers and farmers, banks and casual workers, all impact on one another. And relationships are not necessarily rosy. Their interests and goals are often at odds. Some groups are more powerful than others. They dominate and exploit each other. They abuse their unique sources of power and capitalise on others' weaknesses. In this view, groups struggle to achieve their own interests.

In the punters' view, the market is about the use and abuse of power. Groups manipulate goals and constraints. They corrupt the market so that the grand consumption of democracy is unrecognisable. This view does not see the market as a democracy at all. Included in the array of different circumstances and constraints facing people in different social groups, there are three major ways in which the market is distorted.

Democracy on a sliding income scale

Advocates of the punters' view are sceptical that user pays gives all consumers a voice. They reject the idea the market targets resources to everyone's benefit. They argue that the market is democracy on a sliding income scale. Your vote is determined by how much you have to spend. Rich people have powerful votes. Poorer people are silenced. Resources are not targeted for the greater good.

Consider splitting $500,000 of annual income between 10 people. Consider what the market would provide if one person got $400,000 and the remaining $100,000 was split between the other nine. An efficient market would provide an extravagant home, a fabulous car and exceptional food and clothes for the wealthy person – and basic survival rations for the other nine. But if the income were split evenly, giving them each $50,000 a year, the way the money was spent would change and the market would deliver quite different products. There would be a drop in orders for Mercedes and fancy meals. But medium-range food, housing, fridges and televisions would boom.

What counts as an 'efficient' allocation of the community's resources depends on how income is distributed. For people to have an equal say in how resources are used, and for the market to live up to its claims of being a democracy of consumption, there needs to be reasonable income equality.

What drives our choices

The punters' view is aware of the efforts of political hacks, media moguls and advertisers to manipulate our choices. These pedlars of 'information' shape our view of the world. They seek to inform our goals and mould our perception of our constraints. At one level we have lobby groups trying to win the war of ideas on issues like cutting greenhouse emissions. Different groups try to shape our perceptions of what will happen if we don't cut them, how much the cuts would cost, and what other business opportunities will open up if we do. At another level we have advertisers telling us that chewing gum after meals will improve our dental health or that particular sunglasses will boost our social status. In the punters' view these information wars are essential to understanding the economy. They consider the economic rationalist approach – that 'people want whatever people want and it is none of our affair' – is negligent. It fails to recognise one of the most important underlying dynamics in how the economy works.

In this view, if a sportshoe company convinces every teenager that they cannot hold their head up at school unless they wear its particular brand of shoes and then proceeds to meet that need, it is not clear that the company has made a net contribution to the community. Nor is it clear, despite the company's booming profitability, that our scarce resources have been effectively targeted at bringing the greatest possible benefit to the community.

Or, to take a harsher example, consider whether companies convincing women in the third world to bottle-feed is a net contribution to human well-being. A number of milk formula companies have sought to convince women in developing countries that using milk powders to feed their babies is modern, civilised and scientifically better than breast-feeding. However, bottle-feeding using unsafe water, and where poverty and illiteracy can result in over-diluting the formula, can make babies extremely ill. In 2000 an estimated 1.5 million babies died unnecessarily due to unsafe bottle-feeding. Undoubtedly, when these women purchased the milk powder they thought they were acting in their babies' interest. However, it seems unlikely that this use of our scarce resources is actually boosting the welfare of the community.

Similar arguments could be made about advertising in a range of industries – tobacco, beauty and cosmetics, and some parts of the pharmaceuticals industry, to name just a few.

In the punters' view, the manipulation of information is an essential part of the way groups abuse and exploit each other. The baby milk companies are making considerable profit on the back of human misery. And so, many would argue, are sportshoe companies. In this view, a free-for-all in the democracy of consumption will lead to resources being targeted to the benefit of those that control the information machines. The shape of our economy is dictated by the battle for our minds. Again, the democratic market ideal is corrupted beyond recognition.

The business playing field

The punters' view also rejects that the playing field is level on the production side of the market. It argues that businesses do not start on an equal footing. Relative access to money, crucial information, education and rare skills makes the playing field uneven. Some are better placed than others to grab the opportunities. They can exercise market power, wage price wars and exploit isolated markets. This creates inefficiency. When businesses are not constrained by competitive forces, their self-interested behaviour can run amok. They exploit people and waste resources. Again, the market falls short of the grand democracy of consumption ideal.

A further set of complications

In the punters' view, economic issues are also intertwined with social, cultural and political issues. It is not a straight balancing of material interests. Consumption is not the only issue at stake. Groups have conflicting views on the kind of community they want to live in. Alternative ways of organising the community embody different values and different ways of life. Some groups might think the community would be enriched by some cultural traditions, or that income equality would make people equal citizens, or that moral rectitude and strong religious convictions would make for a better community. Or – religion be damned, economic growth is the key to the community's happiness.

In this view, politics is the only way to manage relationships between groups. Democracy allows each group's interests to be represented. Claims can be balanced and compromises made. Through the parliaments they negotiate a path to the future. Government takes on the role of forging the compromises and policing them. Government should be the protector of the weak and the vulnerable. Part of its job is to ensure that no group has the power to dominate and exploit others.

Contrasting the views

Telecommunications deregulation

The telecommunications deregulation debate has produced a fiery war of words between the two worldviews. At a Parliamentary Seminar on Telstra and Universal Service Obligations in late 1999, Allan Horsley of the Australian Telecommunications Users Group and Eva Cox, an independent social commentator, went head to head. Horsley put the economic rationalists' case, insisting that privatisation and deregulation would deliver a more efficient industry, that competition would improve productivity and drive prices down.

Cox disagreed, arguing that the market would not deliver the best result for the community. She pointed to growing unemployment, the aging population and increasing numbers of people living alone. The community would get the best bang for its communications buck by making sure these isolated people got access to the technology, which would make a highly valued contribution to their quality of life. But, she said, user pays was biased against that. Most isolated people were poor and could not afford the technology. And even if they could afford it, they were shut out of the market by a lack of information. They did not know about the technology and what it could do for them. In fact, most of them were scared of it, she said. Those who buy the technology under user pays are businesses and people actively involved in the new technologies. Young people, working people and people on high incomes would be the principal consumers. The competitive market would not produce the best distribution of resources for the greatest good of society.

Horsley accepted that some people would be left behind by the user pays industry. But government-imposed Universal Service Obligations, setting out a minimum standard of service for the bottom 10% of people, would make sure everyone got access to services. Consistent with good economic practice, he argued that the market should be organised in the most efficient way possible and then free services targeted to achieve particular social goals. The cost of providing such services should be spread across the industry and be funded from surpluses created by the efficiencies of competition.

Cox took issue with Horsley's approach of targeting assistance to people at the bottom rather than governments providing the services across the board. She argued that there were a number of problems in managing the relationships between social groups in that way. Targeting people at the bottom is difficult in practice and creates problems with social cohesion. She pointed to the rise of Pauline Hanson's One Nation Party as an example of the problems created by targeting. Poor white people get angry when they see even poorer Aboriginal people being given things the whites cannot afford themselves. These sorts of problems arise from trying to target any group in need, whether it be single mothers, the unemployed, the aged or the infirm. In each situation there are people just outside the target group. They have similar levels of need but cannot get the assistance. Cox argued that, for the sake of social cohesion, some services should be turned on as a minimum public service to all. Even if Cox had believed the market provided telecommunications services more efficiently (which she didn't), she was prepared to trade off some economic efficiency to get increased social cohesion.

Cox also highlighted the dangers of economic rationalism's insistence on focusing on individuals' interests. Such a focus ignored important community goals and overlooked the fact that communications are central to our social fabric. In her view, the new technology should be used to invigorate the social fabric, again pointing to growing unemployment, the aging population and increasing numbers of people living alone. The isolation of these people and the segregation of our society was damaging our community. It was undermining our trust in one another and our sense of safety. The community, she argued, would get the most out of its communications buck by using it to mend the social fabric. The priority should be reconnecting these isolated people. The focus on individual self-interest would completely overlook this important social goal.

National Competition Policy

The impact of National Competition Policy (NCP) on rural and regional Australia has also seen the conflict between the two views come to the fore. According to the National Competition Council, the aim of the policy is to extend competition to parts of the economy that have been dominated by government monopolies, like utilities, or where competition is restricted by legislation. Part of the policy has been to overhaul trading hours laws and laws that give newsagencies, pharmacies, petrol stations and hoteliers exclusive rights to sell some product lines. The intent is that competition will deliver cheaper and better services. The efficiency gains will flow through the whole economy, as many of the reform areas, particularly the utilities, are inputs to business costs.

The depth of conviction that 'market is best' screams out of NCP's public interest test. Under the policy, competition reform must go ahead unless it is proved to be against the public interest. The onus of proof is on others to convince the National Competition Council that the reforms will damage the greater good. This runs counter to what you might intuitively expect: that reform should only go ahead if it has been proved the change will reap benefits. It implies that competition is not a tool to be used selectively in situations where it is appropriate. It assumes that there is a competitive market lying dormant in all of these industries, with only rare exceptions. The role of the NCP is to unleash that benevolent force.

The NCP view is also that government regulations unfairly guarantee some groups profits at the cost of the rest of the community. 'Recent debate reflects resistance by some groups to the removal of anti-competitive protections and privileges', said the National Competition Council in January 1999. Submissions to a Productivity Commission Inquiry into the NCP said people interviewed during the inquiry complained of feeling under attack. They said that they had to justify their right to their livelihoods.

But these submissions reflected the punters' worldview. National Party women rejected the blanket assumption that the same market principles could be applied across the board: 'Our members were concerned at the way in which a single set of principles would be applied generically throughout the country and the economy without taking into account the differences which exist between rural and city economic frameworks and between small and large market players.' They argued that unbridled competition actually created anti-competitive and inefficient outcomes. Deregulating opening hours would shut small family businesses out of the market. Family businesses could not stay open the same hours as big businesses employing a casualised workforce. They said, 'Deregulation will only increase the power of the already too powerful market share of the major retailers ... Our members want to see an Australia where there is real and healthy competition amongst retailers. They do not want Coles Myer and Woolworths to have complete control over price, store location, product range, quality and so on.'

The social consequences of economic reform dominated a number of the submissions to the Productivity Commission. 'Government must recognise that we, all Australians, don't live in an economy, we live in a society', said one. They argued that small rural towns were centred around their pub, their newsagency and their pharmacy, and local government was a major employer. When competition from major retailers in regional centres force businesses to close, there are no other jobs to apply for in the town. Families have to move away to get work, reducing the critical number of people required to sustain the businesses that are left. Eventually the town empties out and the community collapses.

Conclusion

The gap between central agencies and the wider community on the role of government springs from their views, essentially of whether in fact 'God is dead', and whether human beings have to take responsibility for authoring their own society. The bureaucrats believe we would all be better off if government stayed out of it. Critical of their line agency colleagues, they argue that the world would be a neater, more ordered place if the laws of the market were left to organise the community. But advocates of the punters' view consider that would mean chaos. The powerful would exploit the weak. Resources would be channelled into the interests of the wealthy, either through direct spending or because they control the information machines to manipulate the rest of the community. There would be no avenues for the vulnerable to defend themselves. And there would be no forums to debate issues of culture and shared values. In the absence of a means to collectively manage ourselves, society would be reduced to the survival of the fittest.

Chapter 9

Contrasting views of the ideal society

Why bother talking about utopias? Why delve into how the world should ideally be? Isn't it a fantasy world removed from reality? In fact, ideal worldviews are essential. They are powerful because they are the benchmark. They are the measuring sticks for deciding if a policy is going to make things better or worse. Many economic rationalists insist that economics does not contain a value-laden ideal about how the world should be. But in the policy world, economic rationalism's ideal is invoked every day. It is invoked as politicians and bureaucrats try to decide whether a policy is in the nation's best interest. When the wider community debates with economic rationalists, it is also arguing about whether a policy will take Australia closer to an unspoken ideal. The gulf between these ideals mirrors the gulf between the electorate and their governments.

There are two key differences between the economic rationalists' and the punters' ideals. First, they disagree on what a good society has to deliver. For economic rationalism it is wealth, and for the punters it is a bundle of issues that make up 'quality of life'. Second, the two views have very different ideas of justice.

Economic rationalism's ideal

Economic rationalism has one supreme value – material wealth. The aim is to make society as wealthy as possible. It argues that the market will secure the highest possible standard of living for all. In economic rationalism's vision, this ideal society is a grand democracy of consumption. Through the market, consumers cast their votes on how society's resources should be used. Consumer decisions on what to buy determine how many cars should be made, in what colours and whether they should be zippy little numbers or big powerful wagons. They dictate what sorts of food should be grown and how it should be processed, through to what books and films should be produced and published. Economic rationalists argue that this consumer democracy is the most efficient way of targeting society's resources. The market minimises waste and targets resources where they are most valued. The advocates of this ideal focus on three principles to protect the consumer democracy – choice, efficiency and justice.

Choice is the first ingredient and, in this worldview, is often associated with freedom. You may have heard Treasurer Peter Costello talking about how tax reform will increase choice, or the former Minister for Industrial Relations, Peter Reith, on how deregulating industrial relations will give workers and businesses more choice. Or the Prime Minister saying that selling Telstra and deregulating telecommunications will reap greater customer choice. In economic jargon, 'choice' is called 'consumer sovereignty'. Choice is vital to economic efficiency. It is the idea that no one knows better than you do what will make you happy. The economy should be driven by the choices people make for themselves. Your choices should drive the services Telstra provides, whether tuna should be dolphin friendly and whether we have small shops or big department stores. What you buy reflects what you really want.

Economic efficiency is the second and paramount ingredient. It has been the constant theme of economic rationalist reform in the last 15–20 years. In the broadest sense, efficiency is getting the most out of our resources. In the narrow economic sense, it is about solving the 'economic problem' of how to allocate our limited resources to get the best standard of living. Economic efficiency is targeting our resources to give us the houses, clothes, holidays and cars we want most. If we siphon off resources into goods we do not care about, or if we waste resources, we cost ourselves wealth. A lack of competition, propping up old industries and excessive government regulation are all sources of inefficiency. The view is that a competitive market is the best way to get the most out of our resources.

In economic rationalism's ideal, justice is also intertwined with efficiency. In this view, justice is efficiency and efficiency is justice. Two reasons are commonly cited as to why efficiency is justice. The first is the idea that the market is an impartial arbiter of society. In a rapidly changing world it deals out new 'realities' without fear or favour. The market co-ordinates society entirely on the basis of price and does not discriminate between people. In *Free to Choose*, Milton Friedman, winner of the 1976 Nobel Prize for economics, marvelled:

> The price system is the mechanism that performs this task [of market co-ordination] without central direction, without requiring people to speak to one another or to like one another. When you buy your pencil or your daily bread, you don't know whether the pencil was made or the wheat was grown by a white man or a black man, by a Chinese or an Indian. As a result the price mechanism enables people to cooperate peacefully in one phase of their life while each one goes about his own business in respect of everything else.

In an ideal world the market would not discriminate against people on the basis of race, gender, religion or culture. It would draw no distinction between locals or people on the other side of the world. It would be as free across countries as within them. Lipstick entrepreneur Poppy King backs this view: 'If you want to compete in the modern world you have to look for talent. Talent is the only thing that matters now. It doesn't make sense to have prejudice: you have to have good talent – black, white, female, male, gay, Asian, whatever, none of it really matters. I think competitiveness will weed prejudice out eventually.'

The second reason cited for efficiency being justice is that it gives rise to the greater good. An efficient free market delivers wealth for all. As a result, the free market price is the correct price and the 'just' wage is the market's going rate. A genius football player might earn $20 million a year, and a talented artist might scrape by on $20,000 a year. Despite their being equally talented and equally hard working, economic rationalism insists the pay difference is just. The price reflects the market value of the talent. It directs resources to where they are valued most and where they deliver the best outcome for society. It is just because it is bringing about the greater good.

In economic rationalism's ideal world, government's role would be minimal. Government inhibits efficiency, injuring justice and freedom and curbing wealth. The role of government should be

limited to setting up the conditions that allow the market to operate. Those conditions include enforcing private property rights and
the rule of law. Government might also address the odd market failure. But, mostly, it would leave the market to itself.

The punters' ideal

The punters' view of the ideal world differs in three important
ways. First, it holds that our goal is quality of life, where quality of
life is a complex mix of community relationships, environment and
health as well as wealth. Second, the market will not produce a just
community. The market enables the powerful to exploit the weak,
concentrates wealth in the hands of a few, and does not necessarily
use resources to the benefit of everyone. Third, in this view, to bring
about the good society, governments have to step in and arbitrate
between competing groups and interests in order to protect the
weak and provide a quality of life for the whole community.

Quality of life, in the punters' view, is much broader than economic rationalism's ideal. It is premised on the idea that we are
social beings and it includes a number of often competing objectives. For us to be happy we need to have a good balance of social
relationships, health, environment and wealth. Economic rationalists acknowledge that health and environmental issues exist, but
they are blind to the relationships between people. They ignore the
value of having strong communities and good personal relationships. In contrast, advocates of the punters' view assume that relationships are important. They drive our sense of belonging, identity
and self-worth. To the extent that government can foster good
community relationships, it should. Government has an obligation
to step in to get the balance right.

The second task of government is to police the market.
Advocates of the punters' view argue that people face different
obstacles and constraints. Some are much better placed to grab
opportunities, exercise market power and exploit other people. To
ensure the market operates smoothly and efficiently, government
must intervene – to keep everyone in line and make sure that the
market delivers the wealth it promises, and that the powerful do
not just shift wealth from one group of people to another.

The punters' view of justice is also premised on its assumptions that people are constrained and defined by the groups they are born into. This perspective asserts that the rich–poor divide exists not because some people are better than others. Rather, some are born into situations with fewer opportunities and fewer chances to learn skills. They face the barriers of discrimination, lack of information and lack of resources. Because of this, a just community must create equality of opportunity for the least well off. In the punter's worldview, we have to treat people differently to give them the same opportunities.

This approach conflicts with Poppy King's comment above that competition will eventually weed out discrimination. She believes that the competitive pressure on business will force it to focus on performance, overcoming discrimination. The alternative view disagrees. It argues that people have different constraints on their performance. Women with children have to balance work and family, affecting the hours they can work. Victorian MP Lynne Kosky created a storm when she asked that parliamentary sitting hours be changed to help women with families balance their responsibilities. She wanted parliament to work through lunch rather than late into the night. She argued that the hardship of the hours was forcing family women out of politics. If workplaces don't recognise people's different constraints and proactively overcome them, they systematically shut groups of people out of industries, careers and roles in public life.

Contrasting the views

Debates about student unionism and about tax reform have both played out the conflict between the worldviews.

Voluntary student unionism (VSU)

Key players on the warring sides of the VSU debate were Democrat Natasha Stott Despoja and Minister for Education and Youth Affairs David Kemp. Traditionally, all university students had to pay a fee to become a member of the student union, or student association. Membership was compulsory. The union then put on free or cheap sports facilities, clubs, career services and campus food, bands nights and social functions. The student unions make universities like self-governing communities. Students must pay the union fee, but then they have a right to be on the committees that run the union and to vote for people to be on those committees. The committees tend to be politicised and are the training ground of many of our future politicians.

Under the federal government's VSU proposal, students would no longer have to join the student union, and the union would no longer control most student services. The student would pay a reduced fee to university administration. The university would arrange for services to be provided on a user pays basis, with private companies selling services to students, as with any market relationship.

The federal government argued that the market would provide a better deal for students. It cited efficiency and choice as the reason for introducing VSU. 'This legislation is all about choice ... a lot of students feel that the services universities provide don't really meet their needs. If universities have got to work to get every last dollar from the last student then they are going to be providing a whole range of services that presently are not provided on campuses', said Kemp. In contrast, Stott Despoja maintained that VSU was about 'student control of student affairs'. The government insisted the market would meet student needs better than student government, that the market would outperform a democratic organisation aimed at meeting those needs.

There is also a justice element to VSU. Students pay a flat joining fee and get access to all the services they want. The income divide is as big between students as anywhere in the community. Some live at home, are fully supported, have jobs and are cashed up with few responsibilities. Others are on the breadline. They live out of home and cannot get Austudy. They squeeze a string of jobs around coursework. They regularly run out of money, reducing rations to milk and bread and making transport difficult. Stott Despoja argued that free services give everyone an equal chance to fully participate in university life. Student involvement in clubs and societies, or use of sports facilities, is driven by the desire to be involved, not by the ability to pay. It gives students an equal opportunity to get the most out of the university experience.

The government, on the other hand, argued that compulsory unionism was unjust. Students were compelled to pay the fee irrespective of whether they used the services. They could not guarantee their money went into things they approved of – for example, a women's officer, or sporting facilities they did not use. 'Students who value the services that are currently offered by student unions will still be able to contribute their money, but [it] will now be their choice rather than their obligation', said Kemp. People would only pay for what they used and could only use what they paid for. That would make the system more just, asserted the government.

The final dimension to the VSU debate is cultural. Stott Despoja claimed that the student unions are more than a way of providing services: 'student organisations are an integral part of campus culture'. Student politics is an important part of the university experience. Many students get as much out of being involved in student life as they do out of the courses they study. It is, for many, their first real exposure to politics. Replacing student associations with another mechanism for providing services will impoverish the universities and be a great loss to students' university experience.

Stott Despoja disagreed with the minister on every level of the two different views' ideals. She rejected the notion the market would provide services better than democratic student organisations could. She refuted the minister's idea of justice and she emphasised cultural issues that stem from how campuses are organised.

The GST

Tax reform and the debate around exempting food from the GST is another example of debate about efficiency and justice. Economic rationalists love a broad-based consumption tax. It is efficient and just. It can raise buckets of money for government without mucking up the market. It does not distort market prices. If everything goes up by 10%, it does not change the relative price of things. Economic rationalists think that is great because it does not change the choices we make. What economic rationalists dislike are taxes that hit one product and not another.

First, doing so distorts prices. It makes some things more expensive than others and changes what we buy. It diverts resources into second-choice products. It is inefficient. Second, taxing some products and not others is also unjust. It gives some producers an unfair advantage over others. Businesses tailor their products to take advantage of loopholes. Chocolate biscuit manufacturers decide how much chocolate to put on their chocolate biscuits down to fractions of millimetres so that they get taxed as biscuits and not chocolate bars. They are trying to get a competitive advantage. When you are in the supermarket and you feel like a chocolate snack, the biscuits have a price advantage over their chocolate bar competitors. Car manufacturers have also tried to take advantage of laws that tax four-wheel drives differently from ordinary cars. One company is known to have designed and produced an urban commuter car that happens to be four-wheel drive, so they could take advantage of the tax laws.

The third very important thing about taxing everything equally is that it reduces the rate of tax. The aim of a tax is to raise revenue for government. But government can either tax everything at 10%, or it can tax half the products in the economy at 20%. The broad-based option keeps the coffers full, but minimises the distortion in the market. It keeps things as efficient and just as possible.

But for advocates of the alternative view, such as independent Senator Brian Harradine and the Australian Democrats, it raised a few problems. First, in taxation theory, people can be taxed on what they earn (income tax) or on what they spend (consumption tax). Income tax is usually the progressive tax. The rich have to pay higher rates of tax than poorer people, evening out the community's income distribution. But consumption tax is a regressive tax. All people pay the same amount of tax on each item whether they earn $250,000 a year or $14,000 a year. Poorer people tend to spend their whole income buying necessities. For a 10% GST, they end up paying a full 10% of their income. In contrast, wealthy people don't have to spend their whole income on surviving. They tend to save and invest some of it. As a result they might end up paying only 6% or 7% of their income in tax. The government's tax package brought in a GST and gave people income tax cuts, shifting the balance between the two types of taxes. When Harradine refused to support the package, he did so because he believed it was fundamentally bad for poor people. No matter what short-term sweeteners the government offered, the crux of the package was that it shifted the tax burden from a progressive income tax to a regressive consumption tax.

The Democrats found themselves in a bind. They wanted a consumption tax, because the old tax base did not raise enough money for things like good public schools and education. But they were worried that the tax was regressive. They proposed that food be exempted and the money lost by doing so be made up by reducing the income tax cuts to the wealthy. Their reasoning was, first, that it shifted the balance back towards the income tax system (a bit). It shrank the bucket of money being raised through the GST and upped the bucket that wealthy people were paying in income tax. Second, because poorer people spend a bigger proportion of their wage on basic food, the shift would help them out most. But the Democrats exempted only healthy food, like fresh fruit and vegies. They did not cut the tax on junk food – encouraging people to eat healthier food (and minimising the lost taxes from the food exemption).

Economic rationalists were outraged. In their view the changes were inefficient and unjust. The changes treated different goods and different producers differently. And there was quite a lot of heckling about government telling people what they should eat.

The heart of the conflict between Harradine, the Democrats and the economic rationalists was the level playing field. The Democrats were worried about how an across-the-board tax would hit people in different circumstances. They aimed to even things up by taxing different goods differently. The economic rationalists, on the other hand, were coming from the level playing field perspective and were mortified at the injustice of not treating people equally.

Conclusion

Suddenly it is evident why central agency bureaucrats can believe they are on the side of righteousness, and the wider community can think they are heartless bastards. Their notions of justice are poles apart. It is also clear why having economic rationalists at the helm of government decision making leads to quality of life being overlooked. It doesn't make it onto the checklist as being important.

The central agencies' economic rationalist framework is a long way from being a value-free tool. It contains a view of human nature, a view of how society works and a view of the ideal society. This worldview is nothing short of an ideology. That this ideology is so at odds with the views held by so many in the wider community runs to the heart of the current political crisis. Voters are deserting the major parties in droves as they reject governments that do not reflect their values. Reconciling the Australian community to their governments requires bridging this divide.

Chapter 10

Economic policy and culture

The divide between the punters' and the economic rationalists' worldviews highlights the sources of people's frustration with government. It provides an insight into why people are abandoning the major parties and punishing incumbents with massive electoral swings. But the electorate's behaviour is going beyond disagreement on points of principle. People are not simply annoyed, they are angry. They are expressing sentiments that spring from fear and anxiety. The source of the anxiety becomes clear when we explore the transition from the 'Australian Settlement' to 'economic rationalism'. Economic rationalism is impacting on something deeper than government policy. It is eroding one of the great assets of Australian culture.

The shift is not just an economic change. It is also cultural. Economic rationalists believe the economy can be separated out from culture and social issues. But when we look at what makes up culture, the distinction blurs. When we pin down the essence of culture, the threat that economic rationalism presents crystallises.

I should quickly acknowledge that other major social changes, such as feminism, multiculturalism and Aboriginal reconciliation, have also had impacts on our culture. But other authors have discussed them in detail elsewhere. I want to put them to one side to draw out this under-recognised thread in Australia's cultural evolution over the last 20 years.

So, what do I mean by culture? Its essence is highlighted by those epiphanies one occasionally has when spending time with people from different cultures. You are sitting around, talking and laughing. You've got to know the personalities quite well. You've watched the group dynamics and smiled to yourself that people are the same all over the world. There are people you click with as well as you click with your good friends from home. And there are those you don't click with – just like home. But suddenly, amidst the laughter, you get a flash of insight. All at once you can see that a friend's reality is quite different from your own. It can be their sense of where they exist in space and time or their concept of truth. It can be their relationship to the environment, or to spirituality. It can be their attitude to individual rights, that they don't expect life to be just or that they have no sense of safety. These realisations are startling. They shatter our understanding, transforming our own ideas from unquestioned realities to fragile opinions.

These pictures of how the world is, these realities, run to the heart of culture. At its heart, culture is a story about how the world is. The stories encompass our most fundamental ideas about the world. Whether they are metaphysical ideas about space and time, or tangible ones about how human society works, what people are like and what makes for a good person and a successful life. These stories underpin our social rituals, our language and our way of doing things.

You might be questioning whether it makes sense to talk about homogeneous national cultures, particularly in light of earlier chapters that talked about different social groups. At first there can seem to be a conflict between social groups having their own cultures and the notion of national cultures. However, the tension can be understood as layers of similarity. Because our stories are so complex, there are thousands of threads to each. We don't all hold exactly the same story. In fact, we probably don't share our exact story with anyone. We might share 95% of our stories with our families, 90% with our friends (not necessarily the same 90%!), 80% with work colleagues, 60% with people in our local area and only 50% with the wider Australian community. And perhaps 30% with other 'new' western countries such as the USA and Canada, and 20% with other developed countries. The percentages are only illustrative. The point is that distinctions between social groups and sub-groups can be understood as threads of similarity, and difference. There is no such thing as a homogeneous national culture. Rather, our national culture is made up of the threads that are common to most of our stories. It is the beliefs that are shared.

Some of the most essential threads to Australia's cultural story are so entrenched in our view of the world that they are invisible to us. We don't even identify them when we describe ourselves. But economic rationalism is challenging some of these threads. It is rewriting important tracts of our cultural story. The threads at greatest risk are about people's relationships to government and to each other. To the extent that we are immersed in a human world, it is rewriting our relationship to the world around us. It is impacting on our trust of one another.

The decline of the Australian Settlement

Our old economic institutions, often called the Australian Settlement, established the foundations for high levels of social trust. The Australian Settlement accorded government a defining role in shaping the nation. It was the all-powerful arbiter between social groups. It mediated, moderated and brought together the different parts of the community. Government played a strong hand in protecting the vulnerable. It legislated minimum wages and manipulated the economy to benefit the least well off. And it embraced a broad notion of quality of life for all Australians.

The reality didn't always stack up to the rhetoric. There were dodgy decisions, driven by less than idealistic intent. And the outcomes weren't always that flash either. But, for large chunks of the community, this was the broad brushstroke of how Australia worked. That was what governments did. That was how the world was, and they took it for granted.

This picture was the source of Australian culture's great asset – social trust. The foundations of social trust lie in our relationships to government and to each other. Our trust in government reflects our belief in our ability to pull together as a community and collectively manage ourselves. As a nation that historically prided itself on anti-authoritarian larrikinism, Australians have demonstrated a remarkable faith in their institutions. We have a tradition of accepting what government decrees, expecting it to step in and protect us, and to provide us with leadership, direction and governance that few other societies that pride themselves on individualism would tolerate. For all our loud protestations of cynicism, we don't expect political corruption to go past travel rorts. We accuse our politicians of being greedy, lazy and stupid, but we still expect governments to get it right most of the time. In world terms, Australians have had enormous faith in their ability to collectively manage themselves in a constructive and just way.

At the interpersonal level, the Australian Settlement also bred a strong tradition of trusting each other. We regularly debate the virtues of egalitarianism. We fret about the tall poppy syndrome and wonder what equity and justice have cost us. But these debates have overlooked egalitarianism's contribution to social trust. The picture of a country committed to making sure no one is allowed to fall too far convinced us that we are in this together. It cultivated a sense of a shared future, a respect for one another, and an assumption that co-operation is the most effective way to get things done.

Our national commitment to boosting those at the bottom has translated into a culture that assumes strangers can be trusted. It has created a community that pulls together in times of need. And, most importantly, it has created a sense of safety. A safety that only comes from believing in the generosity of human nature and that together we can control the world we live in. It is a sense of safety that you only notice when it is dashed away. It is a sense that pervades Australian culture so completely we only acknowledge it when we quip that 'she'll be right'.

The current flurry of international academic literature on community, social cohesion and what the jargon calls 'social capital' theorises what the Australia Settlement was doing for decades. It points to the role of experiences of successful co-operation, a sense of shared goals and egalitarianism in building robust communities. The world is championing the value of what we have been doing for decades, at the very moment that we are throwing it away.

This social trust is a central ingredient in the Australian way of life on two counts. First, it mixes with individualism to create one of the world's most liveable cultures. On the one hand, our emphasis on individualism means we expect people to do their own thing. We don't care what others do if it doesn't impact on us. We don't expect people to conform to tight social norms like many group-based cultures. And yet, at the same time, we feel bonded to the people around us. We have one of the highest rates of volunteerism in the world. We pull together in times of need and see ourselves as part of a community. This is a rare and valuable mix.

Second, this mix is the foundation of a uniquely Australian way of getting things done. We have long revered a flexible approach to the rules. Whether talking up the spirit of the Anzacs or watching the most recent television ads for beer, Australians celebrate individual ingenuity and a cocky preparedness to thumb a nose at authority. When this regard for individual ingenuity is combined with a strong group ethos of looking after each other, it yields a potent combination. It is a mix of flexibility and teamwork. It is an ability to think laterally and operate individually while still working towards shared goals.

We succeeded in surprising the world (and ourselves) at the effectiveness of this approach at the Sydney Olympics. It was the contribution of the massive army of volunteers that made the event a shining success. As stories abounded about the volunteers' quirky and spontaneous ideas for entertaining the crowds and smoothing the massive people movements, the *New York Times* claimed that 'the Aussies took the toughest organisational task in the world, and not only made it look easy. They made it look like fun.' In a rapidly changing world, our social trust might also be one of our greatest economic assets.

But it is under threat.

Enter economic rationalism

Our relationships with government and with one another are being redefined. Economic rationalism has painted government as incompetent. The rhetoric is that bureaucracies are slow, cumbersome and inefficient. They cost too much. The private sector would do a better job. Business is more flexible, more cost efficient and would produce better outcomes. So government began to withdraw. Its activities were outsourced, corporatised and privatised. Control of our shared lives was handed over to the market.

Government faltered in its role as protector of the weak. It declared Australian business had to shape up. We needed to be leaner, meaner, more cost effective and more internationally competitive. The tariff barriers came down. In 20 years we went from one of the most protected economies to one of the least. Jobs were lost. Declining rural industries were told the community wouldn't pay for their soft landing. Their supports were dashed away. Urban manufacturing industries, established to provide jobs, were abandoned. The unemployment queues grew. High wages were blamed for inflation. The wage arbitration system that once defended workers' wages was used to hold wages down. The rich–poor divide ballooned.

Governments stopped talking about quality of life for all. Instead, they chanted the mantra of economic efficiency. Public commentators began to assume economic growth was the nation's over-riding goal. When they weren't talking about the economy they talked about education, welfare, and even family life, in economic terms. Prime Minister John Howard launched his families strategy, arguing that family breakdown had to be addressed because of what it cost the taxpayer. The Office for the Status of Women argued that sex discrimination was bad because it was economically inefficient. And after the 1998 Papua New Guinea tidal wave the then Minister for Trade, Tim Fischer, justified aid on the basis of Australia's economic self-interest.

In this increasingly hostile climate, when governments were asked how we would get through these troubled times, they had only one answer – competition. We had to struggle against each other. To keep our heads above water, we were told we had to outdo one another. We were too laid-back. We had to work harder, be more ruthless and focus on the bottom-line. As the restructuring left us fearing for our jobs, we did.

The problem confronting governments is that Australians still hold to the punters' worldview. We still believe that our social circumstances shape us. We still believe that some people have more power and more opportunities than others. And we know the market doesn't operate on a level playing field. But under economic rationalism there is no government to protect the vulnerable. There is no one to curb the power of the major corporations. There is no sense of a community that will come together to manage our collective lives. The world has become a precarious and frightening place.

The politics of economic necessity

One further element of the old Australia has been destroyed by the way economic rationalism was introduced. Previously, we believed we had the power to author our own community. That we had the tools and ingredients to build one of the world's great societies. The birth of economic rationalism came with a vigorously taught lesson that we didn't have that power anymore.

Economic rationalism was ushered in behind a wave of terrifying rhetoric. Rhetoric that told Australians they no longer had control of their world. Politicians used the threat of impending disaster to steamroller their reforms through. Whether it was Paul Keating's 'banana republic' or 'the recession we had to have', Jeff Kennett's 'hard medicine' of cuts to services, or Peter Costello's tight budgets as a ' buffer against the Asian Crisis'. They told us we had no choice. Economic reform was a necessity. They drenched us in a fear of the globalising economy. They had no control anymore. We had no control anymore. We just had to do what the markets dictated.

The words of Belinda Probert, academic and social commentator, capture the new sentiment: 'The vast wage and salary earning majority of us are indeed totally dependent on something we experience as a powerful external force. As our local economy becomes increasingly enmeshed in the global economy, the sense of powerlessness and vulnerability to foreign germs becomes overwhelming.' Once cocky and confident, Australians have become powerless and fearful. We are losing our confidence that 'she'll be right'.

Conclusion

Economic rationalism hasn't completely eroded our confidence and our social trust yet. But, if the rise of One Nation and the 2001 election campaign are anything to go by, it is getting there. Culture cannot be treated as being independent of economics and government. Culture is a constant process of creative destruction. Each day we destroy old ideas and create new ones by the way we do things, the way we relate to each other and the way we explain the changing world to ourselves.

Australia is caught in a bind. The Australian Settlement is no longer viable, but economic rationalism is eating away at one of our greatest assets. Fortunately, there is a way forward. The pressures of globalisation do put some constraints on us. But they are not as great as the 'politics of economic necessity' suggest. We do have choices. We just need to know how to make the economic rationalists see them.

Part IV

Arguing with an Economic Rationalist

Part IV

Arguing with an Economic Rationalist

Chapter 11

How to argue with an economic rationalist

To bridge the divide between the policy makers and their public, we need to have a dialogue between the two worldviews. Exposing economic rationalism's ideology, its values and some of its flaws is not enough. Revealing that it has different views on justice and quality of life is only the beginning. The outcry against economic rationalism has been on for more than a decade. Six years after the Howard government was swept to office on the backlash against it, it is as powerful as ever. If Australia is to make its way past the current political impasse, it needs the advocates of the respective views to be able to talk to each other. To speak the same language. To understand one another. And to be able to work together on constructive pathways to the future. It is only by bringing the two worldviews together that we will find a shared way forward. This can seem a daunting task. But it is not as insurmountable as first appears.

In building this shared language we have little choice but to take on economic rationalism on its own terms. Over the last 10 years there have been countless efforts to smoke the economic rationalists out of the bunker of the exclusive parliamentary triangle, to engage them in the punters' worldview. But the attempts have failed. The economic rationalists have not felt the need to reach out and embrace the ideas of their critics. Convinced that they are the experts, and confident in their incumbency, they have fobbed off critiques as people 'not being educated enough' to understand the great economic wisdom. To make them engage, we have to go to them.

It is important that this language is constructive. It must be useful for forging new ideas and ways forward. It is not enough to simply criticise. As much as I wish I could claim the critiques in the last few chapters were the time bombs poised to set the rationalists reeling, I cannot. The critiques of economics have been flowing for decades. Some of the great minds of the last century embraced the task of digging away at economics' foundations. There have been endless exposés by mathematicians, philosophers, social scientists and economists themselves. But exposing the flaws has not been enough to topple the economic rationalists. The rationalist framework won't be ousted until there is an alternative way forward. Our critiques have to go beyond attacking economic rationalism and establish the basis for alternatives.

And, finally, it is important that the language give rise to a new conceptual framework for thinking about a range of problems. It is not enough to come up with half a dozen new policies that governments should pursue. Economic rationalism is being propagated through the hundreds of minor decisions governments make every day. To truly challenge economic rationalism we need to change the way all the little decisions are made. We need another framework that simplifies the complexity of the world into a handful of rules of thumb. A framework that guides decisions made hurriedly in a vacuum of information. Imperfect tool that it is, the highest levels of government cannot operate without any decision framework at all. We need a replacement for the central agency filter.

My approach

To build a bridge between the two camps, I'll seek to set up a conceptual framework that both sides can use. The aim is to provide some shared turf on which both can go head to head. I will roll out this turf by integrating the two visions.

In previous chapters I described the two visions as being like stick figures. Imagine the two stick-figure drawings, each on a separate overhead transparency. If you put the transparencies one on top of the other their combined image would be a more detailed picture. It would still be a long way short of a Mona Lisa, but it would be a more complete picture. That is the goal of the ensuing chapters. They will lift the economic rationalist market dynamics off their delightfully level playing field and slap them on the punters' craggy playing field. In the process, we'll hold onto the most insightful ideas of the two worldviews and create a better model of how the world works.

There are going to be three steps in this process. They'll each start with economic rationalist tools and then remould them to integrate the punters' worldview. The first step is to establish the role of government versus the role of the market in authoring the communities we want. I will take the economic framework that collective efforts should step in whenever the market falls short of achieving community goals. I will then tweak it to make it consistent with the punters' view.

The second step is to address how well the market achieves the ideal of the consumer democracy. We will lift economic rationalism's market dynamics out of its tidy world and put them in the more complex picture of the punters' worldview. A world where people face sharply different goals and constraints. And where other players in the game manipulate those goals and constraints. This will highlight the gulf between the 'great democracy of consumption' and the free market in practice. It will reveal a role for government in making the real world stack up against the models.

The third step is to recognise that economic efficiency doesn't equal quality of life. Economic rationalism treats material consumption and quality of life as being one and the same. Chapters 13 and 14 explore why the economic rationalist framework fails to take into account this wider array of issues. We will identify what these issues are, why they matter and why economic rationalism overlooks them. We will then look at how they can be debated in economic rationalism's terms.

This approach will give you the tools to barrel into meetings and express your concerns in economic rationalism's own language. And it will equip those in the policy world with a hands-on way of engaging with the economic rationalists and getting them to recognise a broader range of problems and priorities.

For everyone, it will overlay the two models to draw out the shortfalls of each. It will shine a light on economic rationalism's blind spots and reveal a better way of understanding how the world works. And, more importantly, it will provide some insights into how we can make it work better. It aims to point to the possibilities of the future.

Chapter 12

Reclaiming responsibility

Q: How many economists does it take to change a light bulb?

A: None. They just sit back and wait for the invisible hand to do it.

On 1 December 1999 riots rocked the normally sedate American city of Seattle. An estimated 50,000 protesters closed in on a World Trade Organization (WTO) free trade meeting. Patches of violence and looting broke out and a state of emergency was declared. Police in riot gear showered demonstrators with tear gas and pepper spray. The National Guard was called in and a curfew imposed. The city, a wealthy benefactor of the country's strong period of economic growth, was left reeling from the biggest protests since the Vietnam War.

Many commentators leapt to dismiss the rioters' anti-free market sentiments. The claim was that they didn't understand the benefits of trade or the WTO's job in making it work. That they didn't understand how the WTO improved justice in the global markets. The *Economist* magazine described them as a 'furious rag-bag of anti-globalisation protestors [that] ... barely understood what the organisation was'. They were also attacked because they supported a variety of causes. Some wanted better environment protection, some wanted labour protection, while others wanted to protect local industries. But while the protesters were criticised for 'not having a clear message' and missing the subtleties of arguments for the WTO, many commentators could be criticised for missing the broad brushstrokes.

There is a deep philosophical rift occurring about how we should manage our increasingly globalised world. Free marketeers want the

WTO to order the anarchical global economy on the basis of competitive markets. But the common theme among the protesters' disparate causes was that they rejected the market being given the ringmaster role. They did not believe that an unshackled market would protect the environment or local industries, or poor workers in the third world. The protesters rejected that the invisible hand would deliver the communities they wanted to live in. At the heart of the free trade debate is an issue about control and responsibility. It is an issue of whether authorship of our society should rest with the market or with our collective efforts to manage ourselves.

This is a debate about whether, in fact, 'God is dead'. It is a debate about whether there is a natural underlying order, or whether it is all up to us. Economic rationalists and free marketeers argue that the market works almost all of the time. They believe that an effective market will swing into action wherever it is needed and dole out our resources in the most efficient way possible. But those that oppose turning over control to market forces do not trust that a natural order will spontaneously fall into place. They do not believe that, opened up to free trade, big business efforts will be harnessed into providing wealth and prosperity for the world. The basis of a lot of anti-free trade sentiment is a belief that communities' self-conscious efforts at governing themselves are more likely to get better outcomes than leaving it all to the market.

This philosophical rift runs right through economic rationalist debates. Free trade, market deregulation, privatisation and the withdrawing of the welfare state are quite different issues. However, they are often lumped together in the public consciousness because, at a gut level, they come down to the same thing. They come down to whether control and responsibility should be left to the market or whether government should seize the initiative and set the agenda.

Arguing about responsibility

Economics has its own framework for the debate about the role of government versus the role of the market. Earlier chapters went to some lengths to drive home that economic rationalism is based on neo-classical economics. The broader economics discipline provides some basis for debating with neo-classical economists and economic rationalists alike. When economists debate the role of government they usually discuss it in terms of the relative importance of market failure and government failure. That is, they acknowledge that the market is far from perfect, but those in the economic rationalist camp argue that it is still better than government. Other economists argue that market failures are worse than government failure and that governments can fix things. To convince economists that government should take the running on any given issue, you must first convince them that there is market failure and, second, that government would actually make things better rather than worse.

A lot of pundits, particularly from the left, paint government as a benevolent monolith – as if it were a large rational creature that makes good decisions for the right reasons. It is quite common to assume that if there is any sort of problem that government should just step in and fix it. Economic rationalists reject that view. They argue that government is just another system for organising and distributing resources, and that it too has its flaws. They insist that people in government have the same self-interested wants as people in private enterprise and that this often brings government unstuck. 'Government failure' is a term coined by economists to describe when the self-interested behaviour of bureaucrats stops government achieving its goals. This area of economics, called public choice theory, argues that all bureaucrats care about is feathering their own nests and building their empires, and that all politicians care about is wooing votes in marginal seats and winning elections. The theory is that these self-interested drivers distort government decisions. They stop governments from achieving their goals and waste community resources.

The debate about whether responsibility should rest with the market or with governments can be argued out in these terms.

Market failure – the narrow and broad versions

Orthodox economic debates about market failure focus on whether markets succeed in delivering this narrow version of economic efficiency. Market failure is a technical term in economics that describes when the market fails to achieve economic efficiency.

That is, it fails to target our resources at producing the goods and services that make the greatest possible contribution to our well-being. This version focuses entirely on consumption. It assumes our well-being is driven by the breakfast cereal we eat, the cars we drive and how many bathrooms we have in our houses. It assesses the market on the basis of its ability to target society's resources at producing these goods in the quality and quantity we value most. Chapter 13 ('Arguing about economic efficiency') looks at how to argue with an economic rationalist on these issues. It looks at the traditionally recognised forms of market failure and identifies a couple of new ones that need to be recognised for the market to be truly delivering on the ideal.

However, this definition of market failure is too narrow. It is all well and good to assess the market as a way of delivering goods and services, but economic rationalists are arguing that the market is a good way of organising our communities. The benchmark for organising a community is quality of life. Quality of life is a mix of lifestyle, health, environment, relationships, self-esteem, meaning and, of course, consumption. Economic rationalism's worldview neglects some of these key quality of life commodities. In Chapter 14 we look at a broader definition of market failure, where the market has to stack up against the benchmark of quality of life. Under this definition, the market fails whenever it does not strike the right balance between the material goods we want and other sources of well-being.

Beware of being hijacked by stealth

Beware! The economic rationalists have won the debate about government versus the market in Australia over the last 20 years. But they have won it by stealth. The debate about how to set our social goals has been railroaded by technical debates about the most cost-effective way of delivering the goals. Instead of focusing on whether we are producing the right mix of health, education, infrastructure, culture, and law and order, political debate has focused on whether private hospitals are more cost effective than public hospitals.

Public debate has been dominated by how we do things, rather than whether we are doing the right things. It has been flooded with a stream of rhetoric about how private businesses are more efficient than government. We have been told that the private sector is lean, efficient, flexible, service oriented and constantly looking for better ways to do things to improve the bottom-line. The profit motive apparently drives business to new heights of performance. In contrast, the Public Service is claimed to be inefficient, cumbersome and full of unnecessary bureaucracy. By focusing on narrow issues of cost effectiveness, economic rationalists have succeeded in convincing the community that the market is more adept at managing our affairs than government. By pointing to the flaws of government, they have succeeded in arguing that the market would do a better job.

But the question is: a better job at what? Economic rationalists have dodged the issue of whether, left to its own devices, the market would deliver the *right* goods and services. Would it deliver the right level of education to the poor or health services to the sick? There are many things that it could deliver in a very cost-effective fashion, but if it is not delivering what we want, it is not that helpful.

This debate has been played out in regard to privatisation of Australia's major telecommunications carrier, Telstra. Economic rationalists argue that Telstra should be privatised because it would be more economically efficient if in private hands. Opponents, however, have been worried that a privatised Telstra would not provide the services they want. That it wouldn't provide unprofitable services, such as to people in the bush and to the disadvantaged. It might deliver services more efficiently, but they might not be the right services.

Debates about how efficiently governments provide services are important debates to have. Problems with excessive and poor regulation, poorly managed bureaucracies and politically driven decision making are real problems. However, debates about how governments can best deliver outcomes are second order to the basic consideration of whether the community should consciously set community goals, or whether the market will naturally guide us to what we really want.

In economic theory the debate can get confused, because having the correct goals, and the cost effectiveness of achieving them, are both called efficiency. Having the right goals is called 'allocative efficiency'. That is, the efficiency with which the market is targeting society's resources at the stuff we want. 'Technical efficiency' is whether the way goods are made or supplied is the most cost effective it can possibly be.

Beware! Arguments that begin about goals often get sidetracked into debates about technical efficiency!

Modernising an old framework

The framework of government failure versus market failure needs to be tweaked in a couple of ways to update it and to integrate it with the punters' worldview.

The 'third way'

In recent years the reputation of the welfare state has begun to tarnish. There is an argument that, as government has expanded, bureaucracies have become institutionalised. Government has become arms-length from the community it is supposed to be mediating. Big government, some argue, has not lived up to the ideal of community self-government and it is not a vehicle for collective decision making. This failure has left those advocating a punters' worldview grappling for another way forward.

The new approach that is emerging out of this wilderness is often called the 'third way'. This movement turns away from big government. It rejects the idea of government as an alternative to business in providing services. It advocates a shift from government as 'doer' to government as 'facilitator'. The approach is that, rather than having government take over whenever the market fails, it should step in and facilitate community solutions. The aim is to have the community involved in providing more people-focused and just outcomes. Labor MP Mark Latham is an advocate of the third way. Let me pinch one of his examples. Take the problem of overcoming the gap between rich and poor schools. In the past, the economic rationalists have said that the market will fix it, and the left has advocated large education bureaucracies that try to bridge the divide. The third way approach would facilitate partnerships between top non-government schools and struggling government schools. It would require the education community to take responsibility for its more vulnerable members, building bridges and collaborative responses to solving education problems.

The third way approach aims to return power, control and responsibility for managing the community to the community. It seeks to revive the ideal of citizenry, to rebuild social bonds and to renew our sense of commitment to one another. In the process it seeks to give each of us a say in our collective future. Ideally it will give us a sense of authoring that future in a way that goes beyond casting a single vote every three years. If they can make this approach work, there is a lot to recommend it.

As a result, when I talk about 'government stepping in', I am referring to the community taking collective responsibility for an issue. This may or may not mean a traditional big-government approach to solving the problem. In many situations, government may only be the facilitator to a community-centred solution.

God and the market

The debate about the market as a natural order can be very 'all or nothing', particularly if you bring God into it. Either God exists, there is a natural order, and the whole thing works beautifully. Or she doesn't, there isn't, and the whole thing is a mess and we should dump economics completely. The natural scientists do provide an atheist alternative. You can believe in a natural order without believing in (a) God. But if you are not partial to ideas of a harmonious natural order, there is another option. There is another way of understanding the market that recognises a role for us in authoring our communities. It also fits better with the path of human history.

The market can be understood not as a natural system created by God, but as a social system created by people. A social system that has sprung up to solve the problem of scarcity. Throughout human history we have had a range of systems for tackling this challenge. They have been systems imbedded in culture. For example, take anthropologist Elizabeth Marshall Thomas' description of Kalahari hunters dividing up a freshly killed gemsbok:

> Gai owned two hind legs and a front leg. Tsetche had meat from the back, Ukwane had the other front leg, his wife had one of the feet and the stomach, the young boys had lengths of intestine. Twikee had received the head and Dasina the udder ... It seems very unequal when you watch the Bushmen divide the kill, yet it is their system, and in the end no person eats more than any other. (cited by Heilbroner in 'Putting Economics in Its Place')

Human beings have used these types of systems to solve the problem of scarcity for the vast bulk of their history. They have worked because everyone accepted the rules. As children, everyone was taught the rationale of the social hierarchy, where they fitted and how things should be divided up. As adults, they administered the system themselves and propagated it to the next generation. The system worked because there was a shared understanding and belief in it.

The market is another variant of this kind of social system. It also only works if people believe in it. It is dependent on people believing in their role as self-interested consumers and businesses. It needs us to believe that our well-being depends on hoarding as many material possessions as we can, and that we compete against others to achieve that. We also have to understand how the market operates and what our role is. Without those beliefs, no one will behave as the models predict and the whole thing falls apart.

Not convinced? Consider swapping places with a Kalahari hunter. Imagine suddenly landing in the middle of a tribe, and the hunter appearing in our market system. We wouldn't know what tasks were our responsibility or how we should behave. The hunter wouldn't be prepared to do some jobs because it wouldn't be appropriate to their place in society and they would have no idea how to find a job or negotiate wages. Similarly, our rolling up to dinner and trying to swap our piece of meat for someone else's would be a massive social faux pas. We might be branded despicable for putting our taste buds above kinship relationships, above honour, above

God, and above taking responsibility for our place within the community. It would be at the same level as the Kalahari hunter strolling off with a hind leg of beef from the butchers without paying for it. Markets are not culture-free.

Still sounds dubious? After all, haven't people always traded? Let's take a closer look at how our current markets are embedded in cultural norms. Think about the difference between a hospital and a used car market. In the car sales yard we know the seller's role is to get us to pay as much for the car as they can. And we know that our role is to try to get the price as low as we can. But when we walk into a hospital we expect that the doctor is looking out for our best interests. We take their advice on what we need and what we should do, with little question. And if we do question it, we rarely reject it because we think the doctor was trying to rip us off. Imagine one day waking up and getting the hospital and the market confused. Imagine assuming the used car salesman's role is to care for your best interests. Imagine not questioning their spiel about what you really need and being prepared to pay whatever price they asked. It would be disastrous. The market wouldn't work at all. That we behave so differently in the two circumstances is cultural.

But couldn't you argue that the relationship with the doctor is driven by cultural norms and the relationship with the car dealer is driven by self-interest? Social theorist Mark Granovetter threw some light on this issue by looking at it a little more closely. If we are operating purely on self-interest, what stops us from stealing the car? Or throwing the dealer into a headlock and demanding a better deal? Why can we negotiate about the use of cash, and not about the use of physical force? And why, if we don't trust anything he says, do we give him money in the confidence that when we arrive tomorrow the car will be there for us to pick up? With only a piece of paper to hold onto, we expect that tomorrow he will honour the deal made today. Obviously, this transaction is not governed entirely by self-interest. There is a whole string of cultural norms that dictate the rules. They tell us what is the legitimate pursuit of self-interest, and what is not. They tell us how to behave, what leverage we are allowed to use over each other, and the procedures to follow once the deal is done. There are social institutions, like contracts, private property rights and law courts, that reinforce cultural norms.

Economic rationalism itself can be seen to have played a role in creating the social system of the market. It propagates a view of how the world works and what our role is. As economic rationalism has become a larger and larger part of political rhetoric, it has changed the way we think and behave. The impact of being 'taught' about the market is highlighted by a number of studies of students in North America. The studies compared the values and behaviour of economics students with those of social science students. They found that, by the end of their degrees, economics students were more likely to assume that consumption is the most important thing in making them happy and they were more likely to behave like the profit-maximising actors in economic models. They had been taught a way of understanding the world and their role in it, and they behaved accordingly.

To a greater or lesser degree we have all been subject to that process. Human beings have always wanted to secure a good life for themselves and their loved ones. But the idea of what a good life is and how we achieve it is learnt. We have been taught how to be good consumers. We have been taught that 'value for money' will make us happier. In recent years we are increasingly prepared to ditch communities, relationships and even families for better-paying job opportunities in other cities. We shop around, pitching one shop-keeper against another to get the best value for money. We will abandon one company for another if they offer a better deal. As we increasingly put material standard of living above all other considerations, we are becoming the freewheeling, devoid of social ties, profit-maximising consumers of economic models.

Similarly, businesses have changed to become more like the businesses in the models. They always needed to keep their heads above water, but the idea that their role is solely to maximise profits is relatively new. Not that long ago, businesses were family owned and were sources of status and power within the community. The status of wealthy proprietors rested on their ability to wield power and, in many cases, to exercise leadership and paternalism. Businesses were social institutions with much broader roles and responsibilities than we expect of them today. But the move away from family businesses and the rise of professional, economics-educated management have changed the way businesses see their role. The professional managers have become narrowly focused on shareholder value. The more economics-educated the managers have become, the more the businesses have become narrowly profit-maximising economic machines.

The market exists because we believe in it. And the more we believe in it, the more accurate it becomes in describing how the world works. This isn't necessarily a bad thing. If we believe that economic efficiency and material standards of living are important, it is quite a good thing. And some would argue that it is better than believing in the caste system or a feudal system. However, others argue that belief in the market has us looking for happiness in all the wrong places. That it will ultimately make us miserable. We will come back to this debate in the last few chapters.

More immediately, the fact that we have conjured the market into being doesn't mean it works well. No matter the might of the collective imagination of the federal Treasury, their belief does not ensure that the market operates smoothly and produces the outcomes the models predict. Sometimes we act like economic actors in the models, and sometimes we don't. Sometimes the price mechanism allocates the resources in the way it is supposed to, but often other things get in the way. The question is: how often does it work and how often does it fail?

A comment on language

Some will point out, quite properly, that using the term 'market failure' gives the economic rationalists a head start. It accepts their assertion that the market exists and that it works. Looking for cases of 'market failure' makes it sound like we are looking for the exceptions. I concede that point. But I consider it is still important to use the terminology because it flags where the ideas fit into the economic rationalist framework. And, in my view, incorporating new ideas into economic rationalism's own framework will be the most effective way of shifting the paradigm. However, one way of reclaiming some ground is to talk about 'creating markets'. In talking about 'creating' good markets rather than 'correcting' markets, we acknowledge they are products of the human imagination. The emphasis shifts onto our responsibility for making them work well.

Conclusion

The first step in arguing with an economic rationalist is to wrestle control back from the invisible hand. The fundamental question underlying almost every debate with an economic rationalist is whether the invisible hand will deliver the communities we want better than government can. To win this debate you must first convince them that the socially constructed market won't deliver the best outcome and, second, that government will make things better rather than worse. The next three chapters look at how you might do that when debating economic efficiency, quality of life and justice.

Chapter 13

Arguing about economic efficiency

Debate has raged over tariff reductions and free trade, microeconomic reforms, privatisation, and shifts to user pays. Some pundits insist that leaving it to the market won't deliver a healthy economy. But economic rationalists insist it will. This is the first and most powerful place to start arguing with an economic rationalist. It is the debate over whether the market actually achieves economic efficiency. Does the market do what it claims to do? It is easy to get into this spat because it is stuff economic rationalists already argue about. There is a clearly established framework for analysing the problem, and, of course, if you can come up with an economic reason why an economic policy is wrong, the economic rationalist is left without anywhere to stand.

The previous chapter explained that any argument with an economic rationalist turns on whether the market or governments are best equipped to bring about the communities we want to live in. It is a question of whether the market will harness our selfish natures to deliver the best outcomes for all, or whether human beings have to co-operate, plan and consciously author their communities. Fortunately economics has a framework for having this argument. It acknowledges that the market fails and it believes that governments also fail. To convince an economic rationalist that governments should get into the act, you must first convince them that the market fails and, second, that government involvement won't make things worse.

To win this argument, the antagonist to an economic rationalist has to be quick on their feet. The steps of economic argument are clearly established. What makes for economically rational behaviour has been rattled off a thousand times before. Its consequences have all been carefully considered and the arguments rehearsed. The most mundane intellect with an economics training can be a formidable opponent. In fact, the more mundane, the more formidable. They won't be able to see the challenges your arguments present or the limits of their own analysis. As a result it is important to have a clear framework in your own mind for how to engage the issue and attack the economic rationalist assumptions.

There are three ways in which the market might fail to deliver economic efficiency: one that stems from the punters' worldview and two that are recognised in mainstream economics. The first is when people don't act in the way the models predict. This is the most pervasive and corrupting failure in the market system. It is also the failure that economic rationalists don't acknowledge. It is the most important so I'll deal with it first. Second, even if everyone does do exactly what the models insist, there are still a number of ways the market can go haywire. These are the traditionally recognised forms of market failure. Their scope is limited, but an argument waged on these grounds is likely to be the most effective. And the third is when people are behaving as the models argue, and the traditional market failures have all been fixed, but the market still doesn't get it right for the future. This level of failure looks at long-term versus short-term economic efficiency. It is the perspective that, even when the markets are operating perfectly, they are often short term in their outlook and not effective at addressing long-term efficiency.

Social sources of market failure

Economic rationalists say 'market failure' has occurred when the market falls short in delivering economic efficiency. Recall that economic efficiency is when the market achieves the ideal of the grand democracy of consumption. It is when the market co-ordinates society to use the finite pot of resources to produce the goods and services people value most. Market failure is when economic efficiency is not achieved. For some reason the forces of demand and supply go haywire and fail to harness self-interest effectively, creating inefficiency and waste.

The most pervasive and corrupting market failures are not recognised by mainstream economics. The market fails when people don't behave how the models claim they should. Its predictions, of what consumers buy and why, might be wrong. And so might its predictions of how business will decide what to produce, how to compete and how to set their prices. If these basic models have missed the mark, the grand democracy of consumption may be anything but. These instances should be labelled market failures and used as justifications for government to step in.

This is particularly the case if whole groups deviate from economic rationalism's predictions. The market is distorted when businesses or individuals don't act according to the models because they are caught in a unique set of circumstances. But it is a much bigger problem when social groups consistently act at odds with the predictions. Some groups will get market power and will accrue the wealth and benefits at the cost of others. In these situations there is massive market failure occurring. The market as a democracy of consumption becomes laughable.

The argument over whether people behave as economic rationalism dictates is often debated in terms of whether or not people are rational. This brings an unreasonable value judgement to the debate. Chapter 7 explained how economic rationalism models what it refers to as 'self-interested behaviour'. It is often implied that when people don't do what models predict they are behaving 'irrationally'. But recall that the economic rationalist models were describing people pursuing a particular goal subject to a particular set of constraints. When the models don't predict people's behaviour, it is because they have got the goals and constraints wrong. The goals and constraints that economic rationalism identifies make up a part of people's decision making a lot of the time. But they are only some of the goals and constraints and are often the less important issues driving people's decisions. Our economic decisions are deeply embedded in our social and practical circumstances. When those circumstances impact on our economic decisions, the free market outcome can fall a long way short of the grand democracy of consumption ideal.

But this leaves us with a difficulty. If the issues in economic rationalist models and the market dynamics they create are often part of our decision making and part of how the market works, we don't want to throw them out completely. But how do we deal with the fact they overlook such fundamental things and are wrong so much of the time? One useful way to consider the problem is to think of our social world as being affected by (at least) three massive scale systems. One is the market, and one is what I'll call our social system. (As discussed in the last chapter, these are both cultural systems, but for this exercise it is useful to look at them separately.) And the third system is our natural environment. These three systems each contain their own internal dynamics, but at the same time are overlaying each other and interfering with each other.

As a metaphor of what I mean, imagine taking a circular cake tin and half filling it with water. Now take a dropper and at consistent intervals let a drop of water fall into the centre of the tin. The result will be an even pattern of waves initiating from the centre and sending evenly spaced waves out to the edges of the tin (and then bouncing back). This is a relatively simple, ordered and identifiable pattern of dynamics taking place. Let this represent the perfectly competitive market. Allow the water to settle.

Second, take another four droppers of different sizes and allow drops to fall at irregular intervals at four random points around the tin. Think of these dynamics as our social system. This is the relationship between social groups. They are irregular. They interact and bounce off each other, shaping and moulding each other in all manner of ways. Think of the impact zone of each dropper as being the centre of each group. The waves represent the cultural stories each group has about how the world works and what makes for a successful person, and how these stories drive their members to act. It is a massively complicated system. Again, allow the water to settle.

Third, think of the tin and the water as the natural environment. For some reason the tin is prone to having regular spasms of its own. Mimic this effect by tapping it with a wooden spoon and watch a different set of waves take off from the edges of the tin. If you've tapped it from the side, an uneven but identifiable pattern of waves will sweep over the surface. It might look a bit messy and complicated but there is a definite pattern underpinning it. This is the impact of the natural environment.

The point of the metaphor is that it is useful to think of our world being made up of overlaying systems. If you set all three systems of waves going at once, what you get looks like a chaotic mess. There are waves bouncing around and rebounding off each other all over the place. That is what real life is actually like. The economic system, the social system and the environmental system are all working at once, interfering with each other, distorting each other and generally mucking each other about.

The purpose of this metaphor is threefold. First, the fact that life looks like a chaotic mess doesn't mean that there are not underlying systems at work. Even though any one explanation of a single system falls a long way short of explaining the total picture, it doesn't mean it is not operating at all. The grand democracy of consumption doesn't explain how our society functions, but it does go some distance to explaining one set of underlying dynamics that commonly occurs within our society.

The second purpose is to point out that the economic rationalists' worldview is the equivalent to the first system of waves operating in isolation. It is one set of dynamics. It is a simple, clear, quite elegant and aesthetically pleasing set of dynamics. But economic rationalism's complete neglect of the social and environmental systems means that its predictions about real life are often a long way off the mark. Economic rationalists like to think they can separate market dynamics out from the social and environmental. They can't. And their failure to recognise it is creating bad government policy.

The third purpose of the metaphor is to suggest a way through economic rationalism's failings. This approach sees the market as one system of dynamics that is embedded in two other systems. And that the two other systems often interfere with and distort the market dynamics, preventing the market from achieving the grand democracy of consumption ideal.

The first point to recognise – in big flashing lights – is that where the market is distorted by social and environmental factors, the market is failing. It is not achieving its consumption ideal and thus is not achieving economic efficiency. It is a case of market failure and should be treated accordingly. If economic efficiency is the goal, then government should step in to patch up the problems and facilitate a better approximation of the ideal.

Second, this approach reveals where we should be looking for these sources of market failure. The metaphor highlights the fact that the market is embedded in a social and environmental context. Instead of assuming that it will operate perfectly, we should assume that it won't. We should start by looking to see what social and environmental systems are at work, and how they prevent the market achieving its ideal. To achieve economic efficiency, we need to look for ways governments and communities can counteract the effects of the other two systems and make the market operate more like a grand democracy of consumption.

(Any interference will of course need to be weighed against its impact on the social and environmental systems, but we'll go into that trade-off in the chapter on quality of life.)

To test these impacts we need to consider the following:
- Social context – (a) the distribution of income; (b) the distribution of other resources people need to participate in the market; (c) the information flows and holes; and (d) the power in the social relationships between market players.
- Environmental context – (a) the availability of resources; (b) the distribution of resources; and (c) the impact of the environment in shaping the timing of access to resources.

We have already seen the impact of these factors on the education and telecommunications markets. The legal services market is another where ramifications of the social context are well documented. In the free market, level playing field ideal, individuals weigh up what they would gain from buying legal services versus the other things they could do with their money. In situations where they stood to gain a lot, they would pay for the services. This would result in services being targeted at the people suffering the greatest injustices, as they have the most to gain from justice being done. And less court time would be taken up with minor and inconsequential matters.

Access to the legal system impacts on people's lives in a profound way. Inadequate legal representation can have life-altering consequences. It can result in people having to live with undeserved criminal records, with flow-on effects for their employment prospects. It can result in people having to represent themselves in difficult family law matters, getting bad property settlements, and ending up homeless or in very poor housing. Finally, it can result in people not being able to wage discrimination cases, cementing their position of being easily exploited. But, despite the consequences for their lives, people do not behave as the market predicts. Distribution of income, education, information and physical barriers of access to services are essential to understanding patterns of use of the legal system.

In practice, people's social circumstances are critical to their access. Knowing your rights and the services that are available to enforce them is the first criterion for accessing justice. Yet very vulnerable groups, like the poor, new immigrants, indigenous people, the disabled, and isolated women in regional areas, were all identified by a Senate Committee report on legal aid as being particularly likely to be unaware of their rights. They were unlikely to know what options were open to them or how the system worked. So, not surprisingly, they didn't seek out the services.

Second, these groups are unlikely to be able to pay for services. They often go unrepresented, even though the costs of being on the wrong end of a decision are much greater than the costs of the services. They often have cash flow crises and are living week to week. Even though it is a good investment, they don't have the cash on hand at the time.

And, third, many people in these groups have had little education, leaving them poorly equipped to manage the legal process effectively. Their capacity to access information about the system and to make it work for them is restricted. People in regional areas are faced with extra hurdles of access to services without having to travel great distances. And those with language barriers face the problem of needing interpreters.

These circumstances mean that some of the most vulnerable and most in need of the law's protection are least likely to get it. According to the Senate Committee report:

> From the perspective of the individual, rights are not rights unless they are enforceable. The growing perception in the community is that legal aid is unavailable to most people and that justice works only for the wealthy and that the carefully developed system of rights that was supposed to be for all members of the community is being demolished.

It quoted witnesses as saying: 'There is almost a self perpetuating cynicism developing amongst members of the community that they do not expect either themselves or members of their community to get justice'.

Where the free market reality does not stack up to the democracy of consumption ideal, the market is failing and there is a role for collective intervention. Government has a responsibility to step in and make the real world better approximate the economic rationalists' ideal. In this instance, it should help people to overcome the barriers to accessing legal services. Government has a role in making sure that all citizens are equally well informed about their rights under the law and in equipping them with the skills to participate in the legal system – particularly if they are in actions against more powerful players. It has a role in addressing the way cost locks society's most vulnerable out of the justice system. It is only by doing these things that we can create economic efficiency.

Any government action should of course face the basic test of whether intervention would make the problem better or worse. But if the market failure is greater than the likely government failure, it is reasonable for the community to demand that governments come to their aid.

Income distribution failure

Income distribution is the most devastating failure in the democracy of consumption. It is a failure mainstream economics ignores completely.

Since the late 1930s economists have argued it is impossible to compare 'utility' across people. They argue we cannot assume that two people will get the same pleasure from a gourmet dinner. As a result, they argue we cannot know if a person spending $100,000 is getting more utility than a person living off $5000 a year. They argue making comparisons across people is impossible and wash their hands of the whole question of income distribution. They argue that their job is to maximise utility for each individual given their circumstances.

It is notable that this approach to utility emerged at the height of the battle of ideas between socialism and capitalism. Prior to the late 1930s, the common approach to utility led many economists to argue that an equal income distribution was needed to bring about the greatest welfare of society. But then John Hicks published *Value and Capital* in 1939 and the idea that utility was not comparable across individuals was introduced. It let economists declare themselves agnostic on income distribution and focus only on individuals.

As a result, when this book suggests people should have an equal vote in the democracy of consumption, it is a break from current economic approaches. Its argument that the market can only be regarded as a democracy if people have an equal vote is challenging the status quo. The argument that the market will only deliver the greatest well-being for society – that is, that it will only deliver efficiency – when people have an equal voice is an innovation.

I argue that the market needs to be a true democracy of consumption for two reasons. The first is that the greatest total social well-being is more likely to be met if each person gets an equal say in what would be best for their well-being. The second is that as a matter of political principle, all people should have an equal say in how our resources are used and distributed. It is a fundamental democratic principle.

Traditional market failure

When people do act as the models predict, the market can still churn out some less than spectacular outcomes. These market failures happen because practical circumstances get in the way. They twist incentives, distort prices and target resources badly. In the cake tin metaphor, the waves are not perfect concentric circles. Rather, they are jagged and distorted, unevenly spaced and prone to interfering with each other.

In traditional neo-classical economic theory, for economic efficiency to be achieved two conditions have to be met. These conditions are vital for people's efforts at getting 'value for money' to translate into the greatest social benefit from our resources. The conditions are:
- Businesses must price products so that the price reflects what they cost to make.
- Consumers must buy goods so that the price they pay reflects how much they value the product.

Mainstream economics recognises that there are a number of situations where these conditions are not met. Four of these are traditionally recognised forms of market failure:

- Monopoly – when there is only one business in the market and so there is no competitive pressure to set prices at the cost of the product. They can set whatever prices they want.
- Externalities – when the product inflicts costs (or benefits) on the wider community that aren't included in the price. One example is pollution that is pumped into the shared environment when a business makes a product, or the consumer uses it. Because these costs on the shared environment aren't taken into account by either the business or the consumer, the price fails to allocate resources efficiently.
- Public goods – products such as clean air, road rules or defence can only be provided collectively.
- Information failure – when lack of information stops people behaving in their own best interests.

These arguments are well known to economists and should be the first line of attack in arguing with them, simply because they already acknowledge them. A more detailed explanation of these arguments is given in the box on 'traditional market failure'.

Taxing our way out of environmental disaster

Traditional economic theory does see environmental degradation as a massive market failure. As the scientific evidence mounts, it is becoming clear that something needs to be done about the impending crisis. Surprisingly to many, while the unfettered market is blamed for damage, conventional economics has been offering a strategy to tackle the problem for over a decade. It has been timid governments that have been slow on the uptake.

The approach is called externality taxing (or pigouvian taxing), and theorists first applied it to environmental problems in the late 1980s. The problem is that business can inflict damage on the environment, or deplete environmental resources, without having to pay for doing so. For the business, the environmental damage is cost free. Governments might pay for an expensive clean-up later, or the resources and environment available to the rest of the community are depleted. Either way, businesses are getting their costs subsidised. It also means that consumers are paying too low a price for the product – so they are probably buying more of it than they would if they had to pay full price. Mountains more of the product is made than would be if the market price reflected the real bill. The consequence is a cost for the community at large.

The economic solution is to slap a tax on the product equal to its cost to the environment. The aim is to have the price consumers pay reflect the true cost. The products that do massive damage would be slogged with high taxes. Things with a medium impact would be taxed less. And things that are actually good for the environment would be subsidised. It would overhaul our consumption landscape. Some products that are currently dirt cheap and abundant, like plastic bags, beef and cotton would become very expensive. And green products that are currently expensive, like solar power and organic vegetables, would become relatively cheap. The price changes would redirect our spending. They would create sweeping changes to our consumption patterns and our way of life. Market signals would direct us towards a more sustainable way of living.

Environmental taxing wouldn't mean upping the amount of tax we pay. A reorganisation of the GST would go a long way. It would be a shift from taxing our 'value-added' to taxing our 'damage done'.

Short term versus long term

Once everyone is behaving the way the market says they should, and all the traditional market failures have been addressed, there is still one more level at which the market can get it all wrong. It is the debate between the short term and the long term. Our cake tin is occurring in a single timeframe. It doesn't account for what happens as the tin fills with water. In the jargon, the debate between short-term efficiency and long-term efficiency is called allocative efficiency versus dynamic efficiency.

The key thing to remember about this debate is that all of our discussion so far has revolved around how to use a finite pot of resources as effectively as possible. However, when you consider the phenomena of economic growth, you realise the pot is not finite and set. In all the models we have talked about, we have assumed that the primary goal is using what we have now most efficiently. We haven't focused on how we might grow the pot.

The competitive market model that has been the focus of this book is the core of neo-classical economics and most government policy analysis. It is based on a short-term view of the world. It assumes that technology, the population and their level of education and the level of natural resources are all set in concrete. In some circumstances, however, there is a trade-off between maximising what people want now and what will grow the pot in the future.

A key example is with the evolution of technology. Because acquiring expertise and technology are cumulative exercises, there are some business ventures that are not an efficient use of resources when they first begin. But, given an opportunity to set up and evolve, they may become a highly efficient use later. This is the argument that is used to justify government supporting infant industries.

This argument can usually only be used for entire industries, and will rarely work for individual businesses. For an individual business you would have to convince them why, if your business plan is destined for long-term stardom, a bank won't invest in it. They will generally insist that banks and professional investors are in a better position to make judgements about the long-term wisdom of a business idea, and that government is not the appropriate mob to invest in such things. There is a strongly held view that governments shouldn't take investment risks with taxpayers' money. If there are reasons for banks or other sources of investment capital failing to perform this task, you will need to convince them of that market failure. Most commonly this argument is used to justify government stepping in to overcome a structural barrier to the development of a whole industry.

Debaters' rules of thumb

The question is always whether the market is stacking up to the democracy of consumption ideal. It is a question of whether the market can produce the best allocation of services, or whether government should intervene. You are not arguing about whether something is worthy of government funding or not. Economic rationalists are always interested in the question of whether it is more worthy than the alternatives. And whether the market can make that judgement better than they can. To win, you must convince them that the market is failing. As we have discussed, this can happen at one of three levels:

- social sources of market failure – when people don't behave like the models;
- traditional market failure – when people do act like the models, but circumstances distort the market;
- dynamic versus static sources of growth – when real life acts like a perfect democracy in the short term, but gets it wrong in the long term.

Having established that the market is not performing, you then have to convince the economic rationalist that collective intervention can make things better. It is an exercise in government making the market behave more like the model ideal. This may involve counteracting social and environmental impediments to the democracy of consumption. It may mean putting taxes on activities that inflict unpriced costs on the community, or subsidising activities that have unpriced benefits. It may mean using laws and regulations to make sure that businesses compete fairly on the basis of price. And it may mean redressing barriers to developing long-term projects. In any case, you will need to establish not only a market failure problem but also a market-friendly way of fixing it.

Traditional market failure

Public goods are the most commonly cited reason for governments getting into the market. Public goods are services which, once provided, are provided for everyone. As a result you can't use the market to work out how much of the service to provide or who to provide it to. The traditional example is national defence. Defence is either provided to the whole community or it is not. It is difficult to provide differing levels of defence to different citizens, to provide it only for those who want to pay for it, or to exclude people who don't want to pay. It is also very hard to make people pay for it, because once it is provided it is very hard to stop people who haven't paid from using it. Police, systems of law and government all fall into this category. It is also often the case for things like public transport, roads and public safety measures like smallpox vaccinations. Once it is there, it is a service to everyone. As a result, the popular economic wisdom is that governments should tax people and provide the services according to their wishes, as expressed through the democratic process.

However, the lines on many public goods often become blurred. There are a lot of goods and services that have both private and public benefits. These are usually called 'mixed goods'. For example, people get a personal boost from having a high level of education, but there are benefits to everyone from having a highly educated community. It is good for the economy to have a well-educated workforce and it makes democracy safer if we have well-educated citizens. Consequently, if education is left to the market, this public benefit gets ignored and the market will provide less than is in the community's best interest. That is, the community as a whole would benefit if more people were better educated than the market alone is likely to deliver. In this situation there is again considered to be a basis for governments to levy taxes and provide or subsidise the service.

Externalities are the second common form of market failure. This is when the full cost (or benefit) of a product is not reflected in the price. It usually happens when there are costs involved that the business does not have to pay. The most common example is environmental costs, as discussed above. But it can include benefits too. For example, there are benefits for the whole community from children being immunised, or from having lots of people use public transport rather than cars. As in the environmental case, because consumers are usually only taking the personal benefits into account, they under-consume these beneficial products. Having governments subsidise the price boosts consumption of these products to an optimising level for the whole community.

Monopoly is the most commonly recognised form of market failure. This is when one business has control of a market. The market failure arises because the business is not pushed to set the price of goods at what they cost to make. It can set the price at whatever it likes because it is the only business that can buy or sell the product. For example, if one business sells the water that is piped to your home, no other business can get access to the pipes. You cannot get the same service from anyone else, so you have no choice other than to buy it from the monopoly provider. You have to pay whatever price they are asking. In this situation, the business can make excessive profits, consumers are spending more than they need to (stopping them from buying other things), and a number of consumers who would have liked the product miss out because they can't afford it.

However, some economic rationalists do not accept that there only being one business in the market is enough evidence of a monopoly. They argue that in most industries, if there is one business making really big profits, other entrepreneurs will see the opportunity to make a dollar and will get into the market. In this view, the fact that there is only one general store in your favourite coastal town does not mean they have a monopoly. Those economic rationalists argue that if the general store were making a bundle then someone else would come in and set up another shop. Some would argue that this threat alone encourages monopolist businesses to keep their prices low, and close to reflecting the cost of the good.

These economic rationalists maintain that true monopolies only happen in very specific circumstances: natural monopolies, or when there are government regulations that give a business a monopoly. Natural monopolies occur when it is cheaper for one business to provide the service to everyone than to have a number of businesses doing it. This normally happens because of economies of scale. Economies of scale means that the more of a product you make, the cheaper it becomes. For example, a factory could produce 100 T-shirts for $10 each or 1000 T-shirts for $6 each. This counts as 'natural monopoly' because any new business could not compete. If a new player came in and pinched a third of the established business' market share, their turnover would be too low. It would be costing them more to produce the T-shirts than the established player, so they could never break into the market. And it would be bad for consumers if they did.

Imperfect information is the final traditional form of market failure. It bars consumers from being able to weigh up what they're getting for the price. It might be imperfect information about how good a product is or what it does, or it might be a lack of information about what other goods are around, how they compare and what they cost. This lack of information can lead to people making bad decisions that don't reflect what is in their own best interests.

However, again, there are some qualifiers on this form of market failure. It costs resources to inform people. Some economic rationalists argue that you have to trade off the costs of people making bad decisions against the costs of giving them the information to make better decisions. These economic rationalists insist that most of the time the market works this out for itself. They note that when we are making big purchases like a house, a car or whitegoods, we tend to shop around. We hunt down quite a lot of information before making a relatively well-informed decision. By contrast, if we are heading down to the shop to buy some bread we don't tend to shop around at all. We take the risk of making a bad purchase, and if the bread's awful we take that information on board and go somewhere else next time. As a result we don't tend to sink many resources into seeking information when the cost of making a mistake is pretty low, and if we buy something often we tend to work it out as we go along. As a result, many economic rationalists would argue that the market does solve the information problem better in most situations than might appear.

Chapter 14

Arguing about quality of life

The largest public protest held in Australia's largest city in the 1990s was over the death of the Rabbitohs. A football team. In October 1999 about 30,000 people took to the streets of Sydney to protest about one of the competition's oldest teams being wound up. But most of the protesters were not regular Rabbitohs supporters. Most were out there under the banner 'Reclaim the game'. They were protesting about the commercialisation of their sport.

But why did commercialisation matter? The players are better skilled and better paid than ever before, there are more games to watch and the games are on at convenient viewing times. Commercialisation, it can be argued, has improved the sport's product delivery. But this is where the marketers appear to have got it wrong. They have misunderstood what the game delivers. One newspaper said, '[the protesters] were protesting about what rugby league has become, which is corporate and marketed and slick but lacks soul'. Football clubs had once been the centre of communities. Children were raised to be loyal to a particular club and felt part of a football community. When the game became commercialised and got caught up in corporate wrangling, it became manufactured entertainment to be sold to customers. It faded into a façade for getting ratings and making money.

If we broaden the goal of the market to delivering quality of life, the death of the Rabbitohs counts as a market failure. Football is not simply an entertainment product. It is steeped in social relationships. Commercialising it changed the nature of the relationships. The relationships between players, clubs and supporters all shifted from community relationships to market ones. When many of the Rabbitohs protesters weighed up the costs and benefits of commercialising the sport, they felt they had been sold out. The benefits had not been enough to outweigh the loss. The pleasure they got from football had been slashed and their quality of life eroded.

The need for a broader definition of market failure

Economic rationalist reforms are not seeking to simply reorganise our economy. They are seeking to have the market as the basis for organising our communities. As a result, delivering economic efficiency is not enough. If the market is being presented as the model for organising communities, then quality of life must be the benchmark. The market must provide the communities we want to live in. Where markets ride roughshod over quality of life considerations, not recognising the contribution they make to our lives, they should be seen as failing. The failure to deliver quality of life should be adequate justification for governments to step in for the good of the community. Thus, we need a broader definition of market failure. A definition which finds that the market fails if it does not deliver the best total quality of life outcome.

Let's clarify what we mean by quality of life. Quality of life is the broad sweep of human well-being. It is a mix of wealth, environment, health, lifestyle, relationships and personal identity. In the economic tradition, I will treat each of these as desirable commodities we all want. Also in the economic tradition, I will assume they are often (but not always) in tension. We often have to trade off one commodity against another. The challenge is to get an ideal combination of these 'quality of life commodities' that delivers the peak of human well-being.

Existing mainstream economic thinking is aware of some of these quality of life commodities and completely blind to others. It focuses on consumption and targets wealth. It claims to go some distance on health and makes questionable attempts at environmental issues too. But lifestyle, community relationships and personal identity are, for economic rationalists, a complete blind spot. This chapter will look at how these quality of life commodities can be brought into the fray. I will skim over environment and health because mainstream economics is aware that these issues need to be drawn into assessments of 'market failure'. Instead, I will zoom in on community relationships, lifestyle and personal identity, in an endeavour to yank them out of economic rationalism's blind spot.

Some might leap to dismiss these commodities as being in the amorphous realm of warm fuzzies, but policy makers of the future ignore them at their peril. Not only are they quality of life commodities that have been eroded by economic rationalism, but they are also going to be increasingly important into the future. Many pundits have already observed the so-called push to 'post-materialist values'. As a community we are putting increasing weight on balancing work and family, nurturing our intimate relationships, being fulfilled by our careers and securing the lifestyles we desire. This trend is set to snowball.

The shift towards post-materialist values can be explained by American psychologist Abraham Maslow's hierarchy of human needs. Maslow argued that human beings have a number of levels of needs. As our lower-level needs are met (or at least satisfied to a minimum level), we shift our focus onto higher-level ones, which then become all-consuming. Once we zone in on high-level needs, the failure to meet those needs can spark just as deep a crisis and unhappiness as deficiencies at the low level once did. The levels can be summarised as:

- basic physiological needs – food, water, shelter;
- safety;
- belonging and feeling loved;
- identity and self-esteem; and
- self-actualisation – to become all that one is capable of being.

In Australia, as we have become wealthier we are using less and less of our resources on the basic necessities of life. We have money left over to spend on lifestyle and entertainment. Our focus is shifting to higher-level needs. As this shift progresses we become more consumed by issues of relationships, personal identity and the meaning of our lives. There is evidence that the shift is well underway. Depression is predicted to be the leading health issue of the 21st century. Counselling, not IT, is Australia's leading job growth industry. Having someone to help us through these emotional and cerebral pitfalls is the most rapidly expanding service in the country.

It is important that public policy keep up with this shift in community priorities. It is becoming increasingly urgent that we bring these broader considerations into our planning and thinking. They need to be registering on our measures of quality of life and getting the weighting they deserve in public policy debates. However, bringing them into the frame presents a few challenges.

Economic rationalism's great blind spot

Unfortunately, there is a good reason why economic rationalists are blind to community relationships, personal identity and lifestyle. It is not that easy to fit them into standard analytical frameworks. It is a fundamental problem in the way that economic analysis is structured. It is a means and ends problem.

The classic rule of thumb taught to young economists is:

- Step 1: Organise society to create the biggest economic pie.
- Step 2: Divide up the pie afterwards on the basis of social and political values (as long as it does not interfere with market incentives).

As a result, economic rationalists are oblivious to there being any value in *how* things are done. Businesses hiring and firing at will, variable work hours, individual contracts, industries dying, new industries springing up, changing professions, user pays, benchmarking and performance outcomes are all just means to an end. They are a way of making the economic pie bigger. It is economic rationalism's greatest failure that it does not realise that the 'means' matter. Key elements of quality of life come from how we do things. Lifestyle is born by the rhythm of the economy. The jobs we do, the hours we work, the things we buy. Community relationships and personal identity also come from how we do things. Whether we compete or co-operate, and whether we are equals and partners. How we organise our economy lies at the heart of our quality of life.

There are trade-offs in how we secure our quality of life. There is a tension between organising things to achieve economic efficiency and organising them to deliver other sources of quality of life. The next section will look at the three core quality of life commodities – community relationships, lifestyle and identity.

Social relationships

Community relationships and social trust are built on how things are organised. Whether we are talking about the Australian Settlement or shouting rounds at the pub, there is an in-built meaning in the way things are done. That meaning fosters trust and togetherness or aloneness and self-reliance.

Economic rationalists overlook relationships because they believe we can draw a line between economic and social issues. But most of our day-to-day relationships occur in an economic context. They revolve around work, the people we buy things from and the people we sell things to. The economic rationalist rush to remodel many aspects of our lives on market principles has involved replacing social relationships with market relationships. In some cases, the social relationships might not have been that desirable, so there was no loss. But often the push to improve economic efficiency has meant trampling over valuable relationships without policy makers recognising they were doing anything important.

The economic rationalist catchcries of competition, flexibility and transparency are the antithesis of many good social relationships based on reciprocity, trust and co-operation. The changing job market is at risk of slashing quality of life because it erodes some of our most important relationships. The shift from jobs for life to two-year contracts and regular downsizing has made staff a commodity to be bought and sold if the price is right. The reciprocal relationship between workers and their employers is being eroded. Downsizing has destroyed the trust and we now expect employers to be ruthless. And employees with market power are being ruthless back. People no longer have longstanding relationships with their workmates and are ceasing to base their sense of identity on the company they work for. The commitment and reciprocity of the relationships that dominate our day-to-day living are diminishing.

The loss of trust in our commercial relationships is not confined to work. One newspaper survey of people's attitudes to business found that 81% believed companies put profits ahead of people. The complaint that a person has been a loyal customer of a bank for 20 years only to be deserted for the sake of the bottom-line has become such a cliché that people barely bother saying it anymore.

National Party MP De Anne Kelly acknowledged the battle is all but lost in her submission to the Productivity Commission Inquiry into the Impacts of National Competition Policy:

> [recent actions of the Commonwealth Bank] ... didn't cause as much outrage in regional and rural Australia as it caused a far greater sense of hurt and resignation. At a time when combined profits from the four major banks and St George are predicted to rise by some seven per cent to more than $6 billion, these continuing closures underline the effects of national competition policy. It starkly, bluntly and unashamedly reveals the ugly harsh face of rampant capitalism which takes account of nothing except the financial bottom-line. 'Survival of the Fittest' is not a formula for social cohesion, private enterprise or an optimistic outlook for our youth.

People have come to accept that economic interests completely outweigh any social obligations. For example, consider this editorial comment on banks' social obligations:

> The reality is that banks have a principal legal obligation to their shareholders to produce profits. Australia's economic interests are best served by strong banks which are at the cutting edge of new technology adoption and which can compete internationally to help boost national income. (*Australian Financial Review* 8 November 2000)

The push to user pays and an emphasis on 'clients' is also at risk of sterilising important social relationships. Whether people are seeking help in the welfare, health or education sectors, they have become customers and clients rather than patients, students and people in need. The market-based reforms have replaced relationships bound by trust, loyalty and reciprocity with 'client service'. Our innate obligations to our fellow human beings have been usurped by commercial obligations.

But is it a big deal if your bank doesn't love you anymore? One betrayal of trust amidst a raft of good relationships may not matter. But, as fewer of our relationships are based on trust and loyalty, we start to see ourselves as victims in a hostile world. We don't trust the people we deal with. We withdraw from public life. We stop being volunteers and sitting on community committees. We become deeply suspicious of our social institutions, such as government, the legal system and the media. We expect they will only be in it for themselves. We are tense and defensive and our sense of well-being is eroded.

Arguing with economic rationalists about social relationships

In the economic jargon, a cost to social relationships can be argued to be an externality – a spin-off from the market that is not included in market prices. But the cost to social relationships is more difficult than an environmental externality for a couple of reasons:

- It is not a problem that can be fixed by simply adding the cost to the price. To fix the problem, the relationships need to change. We need different ways of delivering the service.
- It is difficult to weigh up relationship benefits against economic costs. However, governments can be guided by starting where the community relationship costs are greatest. The costs peak when we erode relationships based on our innate obligations to our fellow human beings. That is, the relationships that look after us when we are in need. Health, community support, safety and justice spring to mind. If we reach a point where we believe that people will only help us when we are sick, will only protect us or make sure we get justice if they are going to make a dollar out of it, we have done ourselves a grievous disservice.

To address these issues, we need to focus on delivering services in ways that put primacy on our responsibilities to people in need. Ability to pay, profit maximising and competition shouldn't get a look in.

There are two approaches to doing this. One I will hold back until Chapter 16. The second is that Medicare-type health systems offer a model for providing these types of services. In such systems, a lump sum of money is made available and health professionals are given the discretion of allocating services on

---

the basis of need. (Police services work on a similar basis. It strikes me as strange that access to justice/legal services, a cornerstone of citizenship, does not.) Nonetheless, this approach of allocating resources on the basis of professional judgement and ethics is one way we can honour our innate obligations to one another and salvage our social fabric.

Identity

The second quality of life commodity that economic rationalism ignores is identity. Personal identity, dignity and self-worth are central to our happiness and well-being. Again, economic rationalism overlooks this issue because it is buried in how things are done. Identity is defined by the relationships between people. Our identity is how we fit into the big picture of society. It expresses our role in society and our links to the people around us. How we organise the economy impacts on our sense of identity in at least four different ways.

First, in Australian society our identity comes largely from our place in the economy. The economy is a huge machine for churning out the material goods that sustain our lives. Within that great machine we are all divvied out roles. The economy can be divided into sectors that provide the food, clothing, housing, transport and entertainment that make up our lifestyles. Each sector is made up of lots of companies and businesses that fill niches in the market. Each company is then made up of employees who perform different roles in turning out the company product. Our jobs define our role in the great machine that is the economy. Whether you are a bricklayer for the local council, a nurse at a country hospital or the CEO of a major food processing company defines your role in society. Our jobs are overlaid with other socially defined identities. Our age, hobbies, marital status and political beliefs are important. But our jobs remain paramount. It is usually the first question we ask people we've just met and it is at the top of the list in how we describe and rank people.

When we restructure the economy, some industries disappear and new ones emerge, dramatically reshaping people's identities. People go from performing one role in the community to another. Who they are, and who they perceive themselves to be, changes.

Second, how we organise things also affects the status of different roles. For example, in the transition from the Australian Settlement to economic rationalism, governments went from propping up industries to protect living standards, to giving people handouts through the welfare system. The money that changes hands in either approach is about the same. (In economic theory terms, it is two different ways of doing the same thing.) But the social and psychological difference between 'keeping Aussies in jobs' and 'being bludged off' is massive.

Third, identity issues also kick in when we look at social equity issues. When quizzed about justice and equity, most economic rationalists respond that their aim is to make those at the bottom better off. They argue that if the poorest are wealthier in absolute terms then there has been progress and society's well-being has been advanced. Most economic rationalists will argue this is the case irrespective of the income divide. They will not see that the gulf between rich and poor means they perform different roles in society and that the bigger the income divide, the bigger the status gap between those roles. They will overlook the fact that the greater the gap, the lower the status of those at the bottom.

Pro-growth policies that blow out the gap between rich and poor are at risk of eroding community quality of life. Even though the poor's level of material consumption might improve, the corresponding drop in social status may be enough to lower their overall sense of well-being.

There is evidence of this phenomenon in Australia in the 1990s. The economic reforms of the Keating era boosted growth at the cost of income equality. Middle class Australians own more cars and have more bathrooms in their houses than they used to. But, despite the improvement in absolute terms, those in the middle are much closer to the bottom than they used to be. As the middle class has watched the poor catch up and the wealthy streak ahead, they feel that they have gone backwards. They have slipped down the social hierarchy.

These feelings are often translated into complaints about being under economic strain. The struggle to keep up with the Joneses has us all on full stretch. When people around us are richer than we are, we tend to feel inadequate. We push ourselves to keep up and to afford the restaurants, clothes, holidays and cars of our peers. The credit card takes a hammering. And so do our stress levels and sense of self-worth. After nearly a decade of economic growth, for many of us money is as tight as ever, and many report a view that life in Australia is going backwards.

Finally, how the economy is organised is also of cultural importance. The jobs we do, the industries we work in and how we work shape our cultural identity. Whether we are a nation of jackeroos working the land or urban computer programmers changes who we are. It impacts on how we see ourselves as individuals and as a community. It shapes our culture and our worldview.

Arguing with economic rationalists about identity

Identity issues are even more difficult. The status, identity and cultural consequences of how we organise our economy are also an economic externality. They are costs that come out of the market operating that aren't included in the market's own internal logic. Governments, and the community more widely, need to be conscious of their power in authoring the big picture. Equality, dignity and ensuring people have a respected role in the community are the rules of thumb. Issues that need attention in the economic rationalism arena include:

- Reasonable income equality, preferably delivered through wages.
- Ensuring people have a valued role in the community – whether this is jobs for the young or ensuring that older people have a role as they retire.
- Easing the path of restructuring – treating people with dignity and giving them proactive support and something to base their self-esteem on while they remake themselves in new careers.

Lifestyle

Maslow referred to the final human need as being 'self-actualisa-tion'. This sounds rather like psychobabble, but the anecdotal explanation resonates more powerfully. The argument is that often, although you have a perfectly adequate job that lets you live comfortably, the discontent sets in. You can do the job competently, but it doesn't set your soul on fire, and you start to get restless. You start wanting to do something that brings more meaning to your life. You can distract yourself for a while, with the charge up the corporate ladder, plans for holidays and house renovations, and the odd bout of consumer therapy. But eventually you realise that having the boss's job rather than your own isn't really going to improve things, and you become consumed by the boring pointlessness of it all. This is Maslow's self-actualisation need kicking in.

Maslow argues that for people to get past this bored restlessness they need to find their vocation. They need to spend time on activities that do bring meaning to their lives. For some this will be family or volunteer work, for others it will be sporting, scientific or creative endeavours. Only a few of us will be able to make our vocations our paying jobs. For most of us our vocation will be our hobbies. We will fit these meaningful activities in around our work and family commitments.

Meeting this need for self-actualisation can be summed up as lifestyle. It is the need to find a balance of work, 'leisure' and family. Market practices that stop people from finding this balance undermine quality of life. The most powerful influences on lifestyle are the location of industries and work hours. Location is vital. Whether people live in country towns, on the coast or in big cities dramatically affects what they can do. Whether they are near their families, or whether their communities have the galleries, bushland or coin-collecting groups they crave matters. Where we live affects our choice of vocations. It is important to ensure that our jobs are where we want our lifestyles to be.

The other significant and noticeably deteriorating quality of life commodity is work hours. The push for international competitiveness has cranked up the hours in the last 10–15 years. The number of Australian men working more than 45 hours a week is second only to the British in the OECD, and Australian women are second only to the Japanese. The punishing work hours are not only hitting our health and leaving us fatigued. They are also blocking us from spending time with our families, our hobbies or the community activities that give meaning to our lives.

Work is also becoming less predictable. More and more people do not have fixed start and finish times, and work variable days, weekends and shift-work. This is compounded by short-term contracts and less job security. The lack of routine and certainty is making it harder to have a life outside of work. It is harder to balance work and family. The lack of long-term security means we think twice about buying houses, having kids and making big financial commitments. Our inability to plan makes it hard to get involved in anything outside work. It is more and more difficult to balance our work with meaningful activities.

Job flexibility can deliver enormous benefits if it is applied with lifestyle in mind. It opens the door to balancing home and work better than ever before. It lets us customise our lifestyles. While some people have undoubtedly benefited from these positives, many have not. The wave of workplace reforms has targeted meeting business needs but ignored the cost to staff. Debate about the social effects of the reforms has been disappointingly absent. In many cases, the human costs have outweighed any efficiency gains. The net effect has been to erode our quality of life in the pursuit of national growth statistics.

Again, this is a market failure.

Arguing with economic rationalists about lifestyle

Lifestyle issues are also an externality. However, they are more amenable to traditional market-based solutions than identity and social relationships. Here it is a matter of making sure that the social costs of work practices are incorporated into business bottom-lines. Governments could take the same approach to these social cost externalities as they would to an environmental externality. They could put a price on the socially costly practices. For example, they could overhaul payroll tax.

Australia's politically contentious payroll tax could be overhauled to encourage more lifestyle-friendly work hours. At the moment, in most states, businesses with payrolls over a minimum threshold pay a flat percentage of their payroll in tax. Governments could tax undesirable work practices by introducing a variable rate. Businesses that employed more people to work fewer hours would pay a lower rate of tax, and those that expected long hours from a small number of employees would pay a higher rate.

Restructuring payroll tax in this way could be sold as either a stick or a carrot – as a penalty for pursuing socially undesirable work practices, or as assistance to behave in socially supportive ways. There are costs in employing more people to work fewer hours, such as training, accommodation and administration. Giving employers a tax break to pursue a low work-hours policy could be seen as government giving business a helping hand to do the right thing. In some instances, the tax break would more than cover the costs of employing more people, giving 'community-friendly' businesses a head start on their competitors.

Either way, the bottom-line is the same. The tax is about forcing businesses to weigh up the true costs and benefits of their work practices. Currently, they are only considering direct costs and benefits to their business. If a price (or a cost) were put on the social importance of employment practices, businesses could make decisions that better reflected their impact on the community.

Creating good markets

To promote the community's quality of life we must find a balance between material consumption and these 'organisation based' sources of quality of life. Reforms that sacrifice social capital, lifestyle and identity to boost consumption risk slashing our quality of life. Delivering happy communities depends on getting the mix right. But, unlike managing consumption goods, we can't count on markets to balance up the benefits and divvy out a good mix. The market can't balance up the relative worth of the things we want, because some of these quality of life commodities come from the way the market itself operates. It has to be someone's judgement call.

Fortunately, there is a lot of research to draw on in making this trade-off. Over the last 50 years extensive studies have explored the sources of well-being in developed countries. They have consistently come up with similar findings. The key ingredients of well-being are good relationships, self-esteem (identity), and meaning. Spirituality often comes into it, because it provides people with meaning. And feeling that we have power over our lives is also really important (though it is part of self-esteem). But these three core ingredients come up again and again.

These studies tend to find that the glow of material gains is short lived. We buy the house, the car or the new clothes, and for awhile we trot around feeling very pleased with ourselves. Whether the purchase makes us feel powerful, high status, or we just like it, it is a short-term hit and the buzz fades. Before we know it, our happiness recedes to its usual level. We just have one more thing to fit in the overfilled cupboards. Even if we look more successful to the outside world, if we don't feel it within ourselves, it doesn't make any difference. We plateau back to our usual level of well-being.

For policy makers, this should be instructive. Obviously our communities have to be sustainable. We need to be able to pay our bills. But, if building good communities and boosting people's well-being is the main game, these three ingredients are paramount. They should be at the core of policy development.

Chapter 15

Arguing about justice

As the papers report community outrage about industry closures, job losses and massive corporate profits, economic rationalists argue that it is not fair to expect things to be otherwise. They insist that it is not fair for car manufacturers, pharmacists and local newsagencies to have their livelihoods protected by regulations and tariff barriers. They tell us it is not just for Australian clothes manufacturers to stay in business if their prices are undercut by low-cost imports. They argue that subsistence wages in sportshoe factories in Indonesia are fair, and that it is perfectly reasonable for company CEOs to be taking home seven-figure packages and share options. How can they defend this apparently irrational idea of justice?

The economic rationalist worldview considers that the natural order of the market is inherently just. That whatever outcomes the market spits out are good because the market created them. To convince an economic rationalist that governments should intervene, you must convince them that the market is failing. You must demonstrate that the market is not operating the way they claim it does. And in the process you must convince them that government would make things better rather than worse.

Let's pin down exactly what we mean by 'justice'. Justice or 'a fair go' can be used to mean two quite different things and, as you might expect by now, these different definitions are based on different assumptions about the world. Justice can mean:

- *Being treated equally* – this is the idea that everyone should be treated the same. For example, take the principle that everyone should be equal before the law. In this view, people are born with equal talents, capacities and constraints. If everyone is subject to the same just laws, the two sides of any civil case have an equal chance of getting the outcome they deserve. As everyone is treated the same, it is an equal competition and the outcome is considered to be just. This is often called a 'process' idea of justice. The process for getting the outcome is just, therefore the outcome is deemed to be just.

• *Being given equal opportunities* – this type of justice assumes that people are born equal in their natures but are born into very different circumstances. To apply this type of justice in the court case example, people will be born into different levels of education, financial resources and access to legal expertise. As a result, even though the same laws apply to everyone, some people will be much better placed to use the law to their advantage. In this view, for people to be equal before the law in practice, those without money or legal expertise need a hand-up so they can compete on an equal footing with their better-endowed opponents. They need to be given equal opportunity so that they can get an equal and just outcome.

Economic rationalism advocates the first idea of justice. Justice is being 'equal before the market'. This is based on two principles. First, that all people compete on an equal footing. Recall that economic rationalism sees people as identical individuals. It considers that we are all the same, with the same kit of skills, capacities and resources.

Second, economic rationalists argue that the market is a just process. They claim that it is an impartial and indiscriminate organiser of society. That it sets prices and allocates resources to bring about the greatest possible benefit for the whole society. They insist that the market does not discriminate against people. It operates entirely on dollar signs, so people have equal scope to exploit it to their own benefit. Individuals are free to go about their lives interacting with the market as they choose, with the market directing their efforts towards the greater good. When people look for a highly paid job, the market will direct them to work in an area which society most needs or wants. When they buy things, the market will allocate more resources to the things they value most. The market, economic rationalists argue, will co-ordinate society without values or prejudice.

As a result, in the economic rationalist view, justice is treating everyone the same. We should all be equal before the market.

Everyone should have to pay the going market price for the goods they want. No one should be subsidised. No one should have their market position protected by government regulations. No one should be protected by tariffs or trade barriers. And no one should be given preferential taxation treatment.

The consequence of this approach is that for an economic rationalist it does not matter if the outcome is 'equal' or 'fair', as long as the process for achieving it was fair. As a result, if a market fluctuation strips hundreds of minor shareholders of $10 and gives it all to one very wealthy individual, it is fair. However, if government does the same thing, economic rationalists consider it to be unjust. It all comes down to *how* it was done. If the market does it, the losers are unlucky casualties in the drive for the greater good. If governments do it, it is a denial of natural justice.

Tackling economic rationalists on justice

You can tackle economic rationalists about justice on two counts. First, you can tackle the level playing field assumption that people start on an equal footing. Second, you can delve into whether the market is really an impartial organiser of society that does not hold values, make judgements or discriminate against people.

The level playing field

The first and easiest point on which to tackle economic rationalists' picture of the just market is the level playing field. The philosophy of 'process' justice is grounded on the assumption that people start on an equal footing. People have to have an equal go at getting the best out of the process – whether it be the law, the political process or the market. Once that assumption is stripped away, the whole thing crumbles.

It is at this point that we must return to considering whether people hit the same constraints when they participate in the market. Do they have the same budget constraint? Are they subject to extra costs that mean the effective price of, for example, going to university is higher for some people than others? Are people held back by non-dollar barriers such as social, physical or value constraints that place them at a disadvantage? Do they have the same levels of information? Do they have the same knowledge or access to the same resources to analyse information? If the answer to any of the above is no, then different people have different scope to engage in the market.

To rectify this market failure, the community has to step in and even up the playing field. Governments need to intervene to help people get the skills and information they need to be fully functioning players in the market. To make the market just, governments have to give the disadvantaged a hand-up. Importantly, this is the same thing government needed to do to overcome the social sources of market failure in Chapter 13. If the playing field isn't level, and the market isn't just, neither is it efficient.

Is the market an impartial organiser of society?

The idea that the market organises society to maximise the economic pie with a blissful ignorance of values, that it does not judge people or discriminate, is quite attractive. And one can point to examples where it does seem to hold. There are people from ethnic minorities, poor backgrounds or who are young or female who have made it. The economic clout of their ideas has been enough to secure them success. However, as discussed earlier, when trying to draw out explanations of how the world works, it is important to distinguish between the exceptions and the rules. We can point to such examples – but that is mostly because they are famous for being exceptions.

The broader trend of economic behaviour is that it is anything but an impartial scientific process. This is illustrated by some work by Bob Gregory, Professor of Economics at the Australian National University. Gregory has an anecdote about being lambasted by American economists over Australia's Anti-Sex Discrimination laws. He tells how some of them lampooned Australian 'equal pay for equal work' laws, claiming they are economically inefficient and discriminatory against men. Their argument was that, in the USA, wages are set entirely by the market and there is a big wage gap between men and women doing similar work. They argued that, as the market set wages at the economically efficient level, if there was a gap between men and women it was because there was an efficiency gap. Hence, they claimed that insisting women be paid the same as men was economically inefficient and that women in Australia were being overpaid. And, further, that the laws discriminated against men because they were prevented from being paid the relatively higher wages they deserved.

Gregory was intrigued and did some research into the market's tendency to set wage differentials between men and women. He tracked the relative wages between men and women in Australia and the USA between about 1900 and the 1990s. In the USA, wages are set by the free market. In Australia, for the bulk of that period, an arbitration system set the minimum wage on the basis of what was considered to be socially appropriate. Men's wages were set so that they could afford to support a family with a reasonable standard of living. Women's wages were set to reflect their social role as secondary breadwinners who were assumed to be only dabbling in the workforce.

Despite the very different mechanisms for setting wages, Gregory found that relative wages in the two countries tracked very closely over the first 70 years of the century. However, when women's liberation hit, the story changed. In Australia, the values behind the wage differences were all written down. The discriminatory nature of the values underpinning the wage differential was clear. Accordingly, the laws were changed to remove the discrimination and reflect the principle of 'equal pay for equal work'. Over the following 20 years the gap between men's and women's wages in Australia closed considerably.

In contrast, the gap between men's and women's wages in the USA also closed, but much more slowly. The implication was that whether wages were set by the market or by law, social values had driven the differences. In the USA, women's wages only started to catch up as the values filtered through the community. In Australia, the change in the laws actually led the change in values. Suddenly, the economic rationalists' argument that the market price is an 'impartial' and 'just' price is thrown into doubt. The way we distribute our economic bounty looks a lot more like the Kalahari hunters dishing out their gemsbok than economic rationalists like to claim.

That said, this example does highlight the overlying economic and cultural systems that we talked about in the efficiency chapter. Gregory observed that the things economic rationalists said should matter, like levels of education and work experience, were powerful in explaining relative wages among women. In fact, they were also pretty good at explaining relative wages among men. It was only when you compared men and women that things went haywire. This highlights that employers were drawing on the ideas of two cultural systems when they set women's wages. On the one hand, they brought in all the gender prejudices of their culture and their view that women should be paid less than men. But at the same time, and as part of the same decision, they made economic calculations about how big a contribution a woman with a particular set of skills and experience could make to their operation. An explanation of wages that focused only on the battle of the sexes would have missed half the story about what determines wages. But a purely economic analysis missed half the story too.

In these situations, where the market is not an indiscriminate organiser of society, governments need to look at how the cultural system is getting in the way of the market's attempts to achieve the grand democracy of consumption ideal. (Again, note the similarities to Chapter 13.) They are not easy problems to fix. Each issue has to be considered on a case-by-case basis to see if there is any way they can influence people's behaviour so that it comes closer to approximating the market ideal. It can require that businesses give men and women equal pay for equal work. It can encourage employers to employ minority groups, and it can outlaw discrimination. It can also seek to overcome the barriers between rich and poor by narrowing the gap, giving poorer kids access to the same education and the same social networks. Creating the democracy of consumption demands that governments prop up the power base of society's least advantaged.

If we don't correct the power discrepancies, the market falls apart. Economic rationalism's worldview is based on the idea of voluntary exchanges between equal people. It assumes that if two people both voluntarily enter into an economic contract, it is in both their interests. The deal is assumed to be a net sum gain. But, more than that, it is also assumed that the wealth created by the deal is divvied up reasonably evenly between the two parties. The human reality, however, is that many economic exchanges happen between people on very unequal footings. The players are often from different social groups and enter the negotiation with very different levels of power. In a bargaining situation where one person has a lot more power than the other, it is likely that the gains of the deal won't be split evenly down the middle. The person with more power will win a disproportionate share of the booty. The greater the power gap between the two players, the more the deal is likely to end up advantaging the powerful player. If we repeated the process of two unequal players entering into voluntary exchanges over and over, we would expect an accelerating concentration of power. With each deal the more powerful wins a greater share of the wealth, boosting their power. The gap in power deepens, entrenching their positions for the next round of negotiations. In a world without a level playing field, voluntary exchanges will not produce a just outcome.

Conclusion

Economic rationalists' ideal of the grand democracy of consumption can't work unless its idea of justice is also upheld. Economic rationalists' notion of justice as equality before the market is premised on people competing on an equal footing and the market being an impartial organiser of society. When these expectations fall short, the grand democracy does not work. The community has to step in. By giving the disadvantaged a hand-up, we can smooth out an otherwise craggy playing field. We can scrutinise the market and make it impartial. By making the playing field level, and the market an impartial organiser, we can make the market just. Importantly, these are the same things that we have to do to overcome the social barriers to efficiency discussed in Chapter 13. If the market is not just, it is not efficient.

Part V

The Future

Chapter 16

The way forward

The last six chapters have sought to bring the two worldviews together. They have sought to integrate them into a single more sophisticated picture of how the world works. And they have sought to build a shared framework in which both sides can run their arguments and make their case. But that isn't all they've done. In integrating the worldviews, they've hinted at a deeper source of Australia's discontent. And a way of fixing it.

Let me pull together the steps of the argument that I have been surreptitiously planting over the course of the book. First, let's recap on the transition from the Australian Settlement to economic rationalism. I argued that this transition wasn't just a shift from one way of organising our economy to another. Rather, they each embodied a set of values. They created different relationships between the people and government, and people's relationships to each other. The Australian Settlement had a strong sense of our collective ability to manage ourselves and it encouraged co-operative relationships between people. It bred high levels of social trust. By contrast, economic rationalism handed responsibility for managing our communities over to the market. It encouraged people to feel that we had no collective control over the society we live in. And it told us that the only way we could ensure our own safety and prosperity was to compete against one another.

The next part of the book went a step further. It argued that the economy is not a separate entity to culture. It is not a separate system that just happens to have spin-offs for values. The way we organise our economy is itself a cultural system. The economy and the market are created by culture – defined by it, contained by it and controlled by it. It is culture that distinguishes between used car salesmen and doctors. It is culture that dictates how we behave in markets. And it is culture that defines the legitimate ways of pursuing self-interest. It tells us how to act and what we should be trying to achieve. It is a whole system of ideas that informs and controls how we live our lives.

Next we discussed seeing the world as a cake tin. I painted a picture of society as being made up of three overlaying systems – the market, the social system and the environment. Like the patterns of waves in the cake tin, these systems all operate at once, interfering with each other, disrupting each other and distorting each other. All three impact on the bulk of our decisions. And those decisions have flow-through effects for all three systems. Thus, social considerations are intertwined in the economy. They come into our economic decisions. They impact on how the economy operates, how we work, what we consume and how we conduct our lives.

Suddenly it is clear that the economic and the social systems are two overlaying cultural systems. They are two sets of beliefs about how the world is, what our role is and how we should be pursuing the good life. The 'Arguing about economic efficiency' chapter talked about how the two systems interacted at a micro level and how groups' values and circumstances meant that they didn't make decisions the way the market models predicted. But this overlay and conflict also happen at the big-picture level.

There can be conflict between our national culture and our economic system. We can be confronted with two conflicting ideas about how the world is, how we should relate to people and what we should be trying to achieve. In fact, we should see the economic and the social as two intertwined parts of a single cultural system. If the two are in conflict, the system is not coherent and the community is thrown into a state of distress. Expectations aren't met. There is confusion about what our role is and what we can expect of others. Governments, employers and family don't make the choices we think they should. It breeds distrust, disillusionment, insecurity and fear.

This is the situation Australia finds itself in. The Australian Settlement was embedded in our social values and was a coherent part of our cultural system. Economic rationalism is not. The conflict is playing out at the societal level and at the individual level. At the societal level, the transition from the Australian Settlement to economic rationalism has created large-scale conflict and confusion over the role of government. Our social values dictate that government is the centre of our collective efforts to manage ourselves. It is strong and proactive. It negotiates social conflict and protects the vulnerable. The government's rejection of this role is breeding distrust. People have felt betrayed and frightened as they watched government withdraw.

This big-picture disjuncture is also creating the conflict within each of us. We are at a loss about how we should be living our lives. On the one hand we feel that we need the job, the career and the house to be a successful and valid person. But we are yearning for a lost way of life. When asked, we'll say that family, values and quality of life are the things that really matter. We constantly find ourselves caught in these dilemmas. Do we go for the promotion, even though the longer hours will mean less time with our kids? Do we dump suppliers who are friends because they are not cost effective? It is creating enormous stress.

We whinge at every opportunity that there is too much emphasis on economics. That everything is too money focused. Yet we are becoming more materialistic and more career focused. While we turn to television programs like 'Sea Change' that tap into our desire to reject the rat race, we are struggling to turn those dreams into realities. We say we believe in quality of life values. But we are not living them.

The introduction to this book painted itself as trying to overcome the divide between the electorate and our technocratic elite. It described itself as seeking to build a bridge between these two worldviews. By now it should be clear that we are getting at something much bigger. The divide is a symptom of a much deeper problem. It is a manifestation of this much larger task of reuniting our economic and social systems. To get ourselves out of this mess, we need to bring our economic culture into harmony with our social culture. The way we pursue our working lives must be in tune with the values we pursue in our personal and social lives. Our economic way of life must reflect, reinforce and feed the community we want to be.

The reasons for arguing with economic rationalists go well beyond taking a powerful group of people down a peg. The first step in reintegrating our economic and social systems is to have a way of talking about them. We have to have a single framework that encompasses both sets of issues. This is the first and most important task of this book.

The second is to present a way forward. This is very much a secondary task. The way forward should be hammered out in vigorous debate between the raft of groups and interests that make up the Australian community. But, in the spirit of healthy debate, I will add my voice to the din.

My way forward

To find a way forward, we need a cultural system that reintegrates our economic and social selves. We need an overarching system that brings the two together and pays adequate recognition to our many different needs. There are two major hurdles in solving this conflict – the effectiveness of the market, and bridging the government–private individuals divide.

First hurdle – the effectiveness of the market

The first is that the market is so effective. For all its many and devastating flaws, the market is the most efficient way we have found of managing the problem of scarcity. It is awesomely powerful in transforming our resources into the things we want to consume. It has created vast systems that co-ordinate the production and distribution of goods. There is a network, often of thousands of people, involved in getting breakfast to our tables each morning or supplying the computers, staplers, pens and paper that sit on our work desks. How on earth could we manage such a complex task any other way? Old approaches of divvying out everyone a role at birth and having a set of rigid cultural norms about the jobs we are supposed to perform just won't cut it.

But while the market looks like the only path open to us, it is also riddled with problems:
- The market is not efficient if there is not a just and level playing field.

But even when this is achieved ...

- there are pervasive market failures such as externalities and monopoly.

And even if it does achieve economic efficiency …

- the market is blind to the things that matter most. It ignores our needs as social beings. Community relationships, identity, meaning and purpose – in fact, all the things that studies show are the most important in making us happy – are overlooked.

This is difficult but not irresolvable.

Second hurdle – bridging the collective divide

The second hurdle is that we need to overcome a couple of elements in government thinking that have entrenched the social–economic divide. Most thinking about government has taken two dichotomies for granted for the last several decades. First, that economic and social issues are separate. And, second, that people pursue their private self-interest and that it's government's job to represent our collective and community interests.

These two ideas have roots in economics and both play a part in the quandary we find ourselves in. Both ideas eliminate any role for people's social values in their business lives. The first argues that our social values don't come into how we work, how we make things, how we relate to people or what we buy. And the second argues that when something is done for the community, we believe it is the government's job. A business's job is to make money, and a consumer's job is to consume. These assumptions have made their way out of the public policy models and permeated the community. How many times have you heard someone say 'Why doesn't the government do something about that?' The combination of the two has meant that social values and individual responsibilities have been left out of how governments, and increasingly the wider community, think about our society and our economy.

The way forward, then, must include returning responsibility to the community. We must rediscover the importance of ethical and upstanding citizens. This is important not just because the welfare state struggles to do the job on its own. It is also important because we need to reconcile ourselves as social beings. When we dichotomise the government and the market, we split ourselves in two. We have our economic selves and our social selves. The two are separate, incoherent and inconsistent. By not giving each of us community-building roles in our day-to-day work, we have robbed ourselves of the opportunity to be social beings.

A solution

But how do we do this? We can't dump the market. Such a change is not practical at this point in history. The way through this conflict is not going to be a revolutionary movement that overthrows the status quo. Nor is it going to be a handful of new government initiatives – though they will be important. If we are to reconcile our social and economic systems, the change must be cultural.

The market is a cultural system. We created it and we can change it. We can transform the market at its core, by changing how we paint its purpose. We can change how it works, by changing how we understand what it's trying to achieve. And we can change ourselves by how we paint our role within it. These changes in perspective can reek more thoroughgoing change than billion-dollar government policies. Changing the way we understand the market can change millions of individual decisions. Decisions made by bureaucrats. But, more importantly, decisions made by millions of Australians as we go about our daily business.

Currently, all our popular images of the market revolve around the pursuit of profit. We associate it with greed, exploitation and rampant consumerism. It is an ethical vacuum. We blame it for raping and pillaging our environment. We know it pummels the poor and powerless at home. And we don't like to think too carefully about what it is doing to the third world. The combination of this rhetoric and our resignation to its inevitability paints a very bleak future.

However, this is not how the economic rationalists paint it. By pinching some of the economists' ideas and remoulding them, we can come up with more constructive ways of creating markets. And we can reclaim control over the community they deliver. We can view markets as a cultural system for creating a democracy of consumption. A system that is steeped in our social values. A system contained and controlled by those values.

From 'free market' to 'democratic market'

Australia can reintegrate its economic and social values by shifting its allegiances from the 'free market' to the 'democratic market'. The democratic market doesn't exist. It is an ideal to strive towards. It is the possibility of a grand democracy of consumption that works. Creating a democratic market requires evening up the craggy playing field. We need to tackle income equality, create genuine equality of opportunity, and minimise abuses of power and distortions of information flows. We also need to incorporate broader quality of life considerations into the equation. The struggle to achieve this economic ideal would sit comfortably within our broader social landscape. It would reinforce and underpin our social values of egalitarianism and pursuing broad concepts of quality of life.

In transforming this cultural system, we would reclaim control of our future. It would re-empower us as authors of our destiny. The possibilities of the different paths open to us would rekindle a sense of collective responsibility for making the world work. Establishing a goal gives us a possibility for the future and a basis for believing that if we do the right thing the world can become a better place.

There are four rules of thumb that underpin a shift towards a democratic market:

- Relationships, identity and purpose are central to our wellbeing. Their importance should be core to our thinking.
- The goal of every participant in the market should be to provide a *true* democracy of consumption.
- If the market is not just, it is not efficient.
- Where the market fails, citizens need to move to resurrect the ideal.

The democratic market must accept a humble position as a single, subordinate part of our community. In the developed world, material wealth is not the key determinant of well-being. As a community we need to give priority to those things we know are most important in making us happy and our communities cohesive. We must respect the primacy of broader quality of life goals. Our economic lives should be built around the centrality of relationships, identity and purpose. They must also recognise that healthy people have to live on a healthy planet. Protecting these things doesn't mean holding onto old ways of doing things. But it does mean planning our future communities so that they enhance (or at least leave neutral) these core elements of our quality of life.

Part of enshrining the importance of these values would include universal provision of basic services that are not well provided by the market. Services, such as health, that meet our most basic human needs should be provided with a focus on our humanity. This is vital, not because it is the most efficient way of delivering these services, but because efficiency losses pale into insignificance compared to the community benefits. These are the benefits of knowing we are safe, of enshrining our commitment to one another, and reinforcing our faith in the generosity of human nature. They are the mainstays of civility and community.

We must also be prepared to engage in redistributive policies that enable us to set wages and work practices so as to secure the basics of identity and lifestyle. We need to be conscious of creating dignified roles for everyone within the community. Wages and work practices should be set to provide a minimum lifestyle for the least well-off. Efforts need to be made to address the identity and self-esteem issues involved in industry restructuring. A place in the community must be carved out for our aging population as they retire. And the growing communities of long-term unemployed need to be given a stake in society. The interventions might not conform to narrow market definitions of efficiency, but they are vital if we are to deliver community quality of life.

Once we have secured the mainstays of relationships, identity and purpose, we can move to making the market stack up to the democracy of consumption ideal. Market mechanisms can be called upon to do part of the job. We can use sliding income pricing to give the poor, the middle classes and the wealthy equal voices in how resources are divvied up. We can use environmental taxes to make prices reflect the full cost to the environment. And we can use tax incentives to encourage job sharing and lifestyle-boosting work practices. By making business costs reflect the community impact, we can harness the market into delivering quality of life for us all.

We can also use other policy instruments to level out the playing field and take us towards a true democracy of consumption. Measures that address income equality, discrimination and the way information and skills flow to different parts of the community not only confirm the dignity of every person, they also improve the efficiency of the market. A universal education system would give everyone a shared language and knowledge base to start from. And hand-ups that redress disadvantage give people the chance to voice their vote. Our social justice and economic objectives can become intertwined.

However, the most important ingredient in realigning our social and economic selves is that there must be an onus on each of us to step in when we see markets going haywire. We must be conscious of what the market should be achieving, and be prepared to stand up and intervene when it fails. We need to embrace the role of each and every one of us in making sure that the markets we operate in are just. We all have a responsibility to ensure that we have an equal vote in how our resources are used. And it is up to each of us to ensure that power imbalances and discrimination are rectified. If we can create just markets, we can create good communities.

The market won't create a true democracy of consumption by itself. But if we are vigilant in making it stack up to the democracy of consumption ideal, if we can reconcile being a good economic actor with being a good citizen, the democratic market won't be perfect but we might be able to make it good enough.

The role of government

The role of government, as always, is leadership. Politicians and government are one of the chief interpreters of us to ourselves. They author our cultural beliefs by the way they describe who we are. They enshrine those beliefs in policies, legislation and the basic institutions of our society. They set the social justice agenda. And they set the standard in their approach to workplace relations, economic policy and industry policy.

Government acts as a role model in the way they provide health care, education, justice and access to basic infrastructure. They set the tone for how services are distributed. They dictate what is deemed to be 'just' and 'equitable'. They also pioneer models and approaches for how things can be done to maximise the public benefit. They do the research and development work for the rest of the community to follow.

And, finally, they also have the power to set what is deemed to be market failure. They have the ability to step in, or not. They can decide if income distribution is market failure, or not. They can decide if discrimination is market failure, or not. They can decide if having massively distorted pathways of information flow is corrupting social outcomes. They set the tone, and, if they choose, they can support the rest of us to have the courage of our convictions. If they choose.

Fortunately, if they don't, we can start without them.

Chapter 17

Making sure 'she'll be right'

'Australia needs leadership, not cowardice veiled as pragmatism', shouted out a woman in the audience at a Republican conference in Canberra in 1999. The audience roared in approval. The comment resonated with people's frustrations with Australian politics. In the race for a new vision, the difference between leadership and pragmatism will be crucial. Pragmatism is the art of recognising the existing constraints and finding solutions within existing boundaries. Leadership is questioning the existing boundaries and disregarding unnecessary constraints to open up new possibilities. It is about identifying the parts of conventional wisdom that don't apply anymore, that never applied or that can be sidestepped. The party that breaks the Australian drift will be the one that shrugs off the 'politics of economic necessity'. It will be the party that escapes the inhibiting conventional wisdom of the last 20 years and paints a future for Australia that offers the values we are yearning for.

We must have robust debates about how we manage our economy because ultimately they are not simply about interest rates and GDP (gross domestic product) growth. They are about the Australia we want to live in. Our old economic institutions underpinned a unique combination of social values, creating an unusual mix of social trust, individualism and a focus on private quality of life. These traits have been defining of the Australian way of life. They underpin our mix of cohesion and tolerance. They are the basis of the 'she'll be right' ethos. And they yielded very effective ways of working together and getting things done.

As our economy transforms, so does our culture. A survey of the current boom leaves the superficial impression of an Australia much like that in the Settlement boom of the 1950s and 1960s. A strong resources sector is again holding up our economy. Headline growth rates are strong. Worker productivity and wage growth has returned to old levels. But while the 1950s and 1960s produced 1–2% unemployment and a modest gap between the lowest and highest wage earners, the current era is different.

The Australian economy, and with it the structure of Australian communities, has been transformed. When we delve beneath the headline statistics a new picture of Australia emerges. Unemployment statistics that count one hour's work a week as a job cloak the size of the change. The proportion of working-aged men in full-time work has dropped from highs of 87% in the 1970s to 67% in 2003. Some of the displaced men are studying, but many are scraping by on part-time work or welfare benefits. For those who do have full-time jobs, the divide between high-wage jobs and low-wage jobs has ballooned. Between 1986 and 2001 the wages of high-income earners have increased at four times the rate of low-income earners. The Australian tradition of egalitarianism is melting away.

Nonetheless, in pondering how to organise our economy to reinforce our values, it is not enough to cling to the past. The old Australian Settlement had limits and will not provide a foundation for the years ahead. Climate change is set to test our prospects of relying on the primary sector. The impact of technology and trade liberalisation has deepened wage divides between high and low skilled workers. We, like much of the globe, must ready ourselves to take on a brave new world. The future presents radical challenges and we need new strategies to tackle it.

In embracing these challenges we need to reject the 'politics of economic necessity' and acknowledge we have choices. Economic rationalism is not an ideology-free science leading us down an inevitable path to a liberalised pure-market economy. Economic rationalism is a worldview with beliefs about how economies work, and about the society we should be aspiring to. It has entrenched ideas about human nature, about markets and about what makes up the good life. After two decades of reforms it has delivered economic growth that is on a par with the heyday of the Australian Settlement. But the distribution of that prosperity is significantly different. It is an economic and social system, and we have a choice.

As we face the future, our leaders must challenge economic rationalists' narrowly focused policy prescriptions. They need to open up their thinking to how our approach to the economy impacts on our values, our culture and our quality of life. In this new century, economic policy must return to focusing on building the communities we want to live in.

Chapter 18

Recent developments: The values divide in industrial relations reform

The Tree of Knowledge, the symbolic birthplace of the labour movement, was pronounced dead in 2006. The 200-year-old ghost gum stood in the main street of Barcaldine in western Queensland. In 1891 shearers met under the boughs of the tree in the Great Shearer's Strike. They stood under the tree to plan the march that saw 3000 shearers take to the streets under the Eureka flag to protest poor working conditions and low wages. As the last-wave industrial relations laws came into effect the tree was deliberately poisoned. It was a symbolic gesture that marked the end of the labour movement and the end of an era for Australia.

The Howard years have, mostly, been marked by a creeping tide. The government has implemented its agenda inch by inch. It has surreptitiously gone about its economic policy reforms. It has made few sweeping symbolic gestures. The great exception has been its industrial relations policy. The government was bursting with pride as it pushed through its WorkChoices legislation. The Prime Minister declared, 'There has been a historic shift in this country over the last decade, and there can be no turning back, our economy has changed forever as a result of industrial relations de-regulation.'

The wage arbitration system was one of the cornerstones of the Australian Settlement. It was the institutional foundation of the commitment to high wages and quality of life for working people. It had been central to the strategy of building the workers' paradise to lure immigrants across the water. It was seminal to Australia's unique mix of individualist and egalitarian culture. It was also one of the first issues to come into economic rationalists' sights.

Labour market de-regulation has been a catchcry of economic reform. The rhetoric has promised flexibility, increased productivity and lower unemployment. Its champions have declared it the silver bullet to transform the economy. Yet the efficiency mantra makes many uneasy. Flexibility sounds like insecurity. Increased productivity like declining work conditions. And de-regulated competition sparks fear of a Darwinian power struggle. So what are the ideas behind the rhetoric and what does de-regulation really mean?

Labour markets are a messy business, so we will tackle them in three steps. First, we will look at how economic rationalists believe labour markets work. We will explore their take on the basic dynamics which dictate wage levels and employment levels. Second, we will delve into the three basic systems for setting wages: wage arbitration, enterprise bargaining and individual contracts. Finally, for most of the last 20 years Australia has used a mix of the three systems. The mix has shifted radically in recent years. An overview of the history gives an insight into the values drift at work.

How labour markets work

Economic rationalists argue that labour markets work in much the same way as any other market. Bosses make a trade-off between what they get and what it costs. They decide whether to take on more workers by weighing up the boost to revenue from having an extra worker and the cost of the worker's wages. When wages are low, the trade-off is more likely to come down in favour of taking on more workers. As a result, the equation we often hear is low wages will lead to lots of jobs.

On the other hand, economic rationalists argue that when there are labour market shortages, employers will compete against one another to win workers. They will bid up the wage rate and conditions. The result, they argue, is that wages will settle on a going rate that leads to full employment.

The competing worldviews

The economic rationalists' view about how wages and conditions are set is hotly contested. The traditional divide between economic rationalists and punters was all about power and profits.

There are two crucial assumptions in the economic rationalists' argument. First, economic rationalists assume that businesses make just enough profit to keep their heads above water. They argue that by the time businesses pay wages and their other bills there is just enough left over to pay the market's return rate on capital. If a business makes a bigger profit than that, competitors will see an opportunity and come into the market. The new start-ups will then compete away the profits. The competitive market, they argue, keeps businesses on a knife edge of profitability. It means that any rise in wages will result in a loss of jobs.

Second, they assume that workers are their bosses' equals. Economic rationalists tend to overlook power divides between people. They expect a worker can head into a negotiation and get a fair deal in an over-the-desk encounter with their boss. They assume that workers will know what the going rate is, and be able to push their wages up to the market wage rate.

In contrast, in the punters' view, businesses make substantial profits and the power imbalance between bosses and their workers makes it hard for workers to win their share. They argue that a worker produces a good and the business sells it. The revenue is then divvied up with the bulk going to senior management and into profits and only a modest amount going to workers in wages. They argue that the power imbalance makes it near impossible for workers to win a reasonable deal. For them, regulating higher wages is about getting a fairer distribution of the booty.

The challenges in how we organise labour markets arise because both stories have an element of truth. Some businesses are just holding their heads above water. They would struggle to absorb an increase in wages. On the other hand, skyrocketing executive salaries suggest that in some businesses at least, the big end of town is getting more than their fair share.

The question of workers and bosses negotiating power is similarly spread. The recent skills shortage is pushing wages up in some industries. Workers with construction trades, IT skills and health training have bargaining power and are using it to their advantage. On the other hand, there are workers at the low-skilled end of the economy with little bargaining power. The class divide between them and their bosses is enormous, and there are plenty of others queuing up to do the job.

The task of managing labour markets is to offer solutions that reflect all this diversity.

Three models for setting wages and conditions

Australia has thrown up three basic models for regulating wages and working conditions. The rhetoric of 'regulation versus de-regulation' is not that helpful in understanding the divide between them. Working conditions are always regulated by rules. The rules dictate what time we turn up to work, what time we go home, what work we do, what our sick and holiday entitlements are, and what we get paid. These are strong social institutions that co-ordinate the way people work together. Workplaces could not function without them. The real difference between systems is not about more or less rules. It is about how the rules are set. It is about who has the power and what their priorities are in setting conditions. The different systems Australia has used divvy up power and priorities quite differently.

Wage arbitration

The first system is wage arbitration. In this system workers are encouraged to band together in unions and collectively campaign for wages and conditions. The collective action is a strategy for evening up the playing field between workers and their bosses. The equal power of unions and businesses sets the scene for a clash of titans. There is scope for serious conflict and stand-offs. A system of wage arbitration is then used to smooth out the conflict. Unions and businesses compete to influence a centralised independent government authority.

This independent authority oversees a system of occupation-based awards. People working in each sector have jobs that are classified into different types. Wages and conditions are set for each job type. The government authority arbitrates conflict between the unions and bosses and sets wages primarily on the basis of an appropriate living wage and working conditions that secure a quality of life.

Once wages and conditions are set, bosses then have to organise their businesses around knowing the set costs and conditions of workers.

Enterprise bargaining

The second system is enterprise bargaining. In enterprise bargaining each business has one union and it negotiates unique pay and conditions for that business' workers. This is a shift from organising pay and conditions around what workers need to organising pay and conditions around what a business needs.

Enterprise bargaining shifts the power balance in the boss' favour. Workplace rules go from being set by a government authority to being set inside the business. When workers want a pay rise they have to negotiate with their superiors. Yet workers still have the protection of bargaining collectively.

Individual contracts

The third system is individual contracts between employers and employees. In this system employers and employees negotiate their own individual agreement. In many circumstances this allows the employer to set the terms and conditions of employment. A worker will simply have to accept what is offered if they take the position. These terms and conditions are likely to centre around the business' needs. In some circumstances, such as skill shortages, employees will have considerable bargaining power. They may be able to insist on pay and conditions that suit them and their lifestyle.

The values debates

People have different views on the wage-setting systems because they have different priorities in life. They differ in their views about what is important and what should be the central focus of the system.

The first point of contention is whether the industrial relations system should be centred on delivering the workers' quality of life or boosting business profits. The question is whether workers' pay and conditions should be set at a community standard for businesses to work around. Or whether people's working lives should be shifted and moulded to meet the competitive demands of the evolving global economy. What is the more important contributor to quality of life? Is it the daily routines of home and family? Or is it the fatter pay packets from more profitable businesses? The wage arbitration system prioritises quality of life, while enterprise bargaining and individual contracts lean towards business needs.

The second point of contention is the way the industrial relations system deals with the trade-off between protecting the vulnerable and maintaining flexibility. Some people argue that the central focus should be on protecting the vulnerable. They believe that the Australian workforce landscape is marked by a gaping power divide. They see a world of powerful bosses and vulnerable workers. To them, evening up the playing field and ensuring equality for all is a high priority. Its importance goes beyond evening up the dollars. In their minds, having more equal relationships strengthens a community and is a boost to quality of life in itself.

However, others see the world differently. They see people as equal individuals. They believe that the average person can walk into a workplace and if the boss doesn't offer a deal worth having they can walk away. Advocates of this view tend to highlight the importance of the individual having the flexibility to head into the corner office and negotiate a deal that suits them. They assume that people have the power to stand up for themselves, and argue that they should have the flexibility to knock out the deal they want. In this debate the wage arbitration system is deemed to protect the vulnerable, while individual contracts focus on flexibility. Enterprise bargaining lies somewhere in between.

The third point of contention is over how human beings really work together. While the economic rationalists assume one-on-one negotiations give everyone the best outcome, others are not so sure. Economic rationalists assume relationships are straightforward things. They assume people will assert their interests effectively, meet an agreeable compromise and maintain good relationships afterwards. But for many, one-on-one deals are good in theory but not in practice. They are time intensive, relationship fraying and potentially disruptive to workplace morale.

While economic rationalists see external regulations as restrictive, others see them as a social institution that helps govern relationships more smoothly. They argue that wage arbitration directs conflict outside the business, and creates certainty around terms and conditions. In this perspective, the added flexibility of enterprise agreements has to be traded off with the costs of the negotiating process. The hours of meetings, the conflict and the fragmentation of the workplace have to be weighed against any gains.

Individual contracts can face the same set of challenges. Some argue that negotiating one-on-one with a whole workforce is an administrative burden. They suggest it risks damaging workplace morale. Many businesses prefer to make collective agreements with unions.

However, in individual contracts another factor comes into the mix. Some big business advocates of individual contracts cite reduced industrial conflict as one of their goals. Under individual contracts, workers have less negotiating power. Their scope for resistance is also less. There can be no strikes or go-slow industrial actions. If workers are embittered, they have less scope to act on it in an organised way.

As a result, in this debate there are multiple positions. There are two schools of thought lining up to oppose economic rationalists' benign take on human relations. But they are divided on the best way to resolve social conflict. Some argue that unions and wage regulation are social institutions for smoothing out conflict with justice. They argue that fairness is the most effective path to workplace harmony. Others reject that view. They argue that the best way to limit industrial strife is to increase the power of bosses and reduce workers' scope for resistance. They push for individual contracts because they strip away workers' ability to fight back.

With these debates in mind, we now turn to a quick overview of industrial relations history in Australia. As the industrial relations system has shifted, there has been a drift in values and priorities.

Productivity or cost shift?

Labour market flexibility is often linked to an improvement in businesses' bottom-line. But before we hail the increase in profits it is important to distinguish between a productivity gain and a cost shift onto workers and their families. If a business and a worker can find a new way of working together that is win–win for them both, it is a productivity gain. This might be working hours that fit with childcare arrangements, combining work and study, or working from home.

However, more 'productive' arrangements can just mean a win for employers and a loss for employees. If a worker is sent home when work is quiet, there is no net social gain. The business profits might be boosted by not having to pay the extra wages, but it comes at a cost to the family's weekly budget. Similarly, if employees put in longer hours for the same pay, it is also not a productivity gain. It is a cost shift as employees reduce their quality of life in order to boost the boss' bottom-line. The hike in profits might make the statistics look good, but there has been no net gain to Australians' quality of life.

When talking about the benefits of flexibility it is important to make sure business risk is not just being off-loaded onto the most vulnerable workers.

A brief overview of industrial relations history

Australia's industrial relations system was forged in the fire of class warfare. Through the early 1900s the divide between workers and their bosses was the dominant theme of politics. The two were painted as being in an epic struggle to win their share of business profits. From a basis of extremely poor wages and conditions, workers formed into unions and went into battle. The struggles were hard fought. Extended strikes took huge tolls on workers' families and bosses alike. The arbitration system and centralised wage fixing were introduced to smooth the conflict. The introduction of an umpire and a commitment to fair outcomes for workers eased the industrial strife.

The wage arbitration system, as we came to know it, was built up slowly over the course of the century. The unions worked through the system to create the working conditions of today. They won the 38-hour week and pay loadings for evenings, nights and weekends. In 1941 one week of annual leave became standard, in 1946 it was upped to two weeks, in 1963 to three weeks and in 1973 to four weeks. They secured entitlements to sick leave. They also fought to have protective clothing and equipment provided by employers, occupational health and safety laws, and compensation for workplace injuries.

The unions were not always squeaky clean. Some were accused of thuggery and bullyboy tactics. At times they seemed to go in for fickle flexing of industrial muscle. In the late 1960s and early 1970s the union movement joined with a number of the social movements of the time and became more militant. Strikes escalated. Over the course of the 1970s a growing number of Australians thought the unions had too much power.

In the 1980s the Hawke/Keating government came to power gripped with reformist zeal. The economic rationalists' sights were set on the wage arbitration system. A raft of reforms were introduced during the late 1980s and early 1990s. They radically changed the industrial relations landscape.

The new system was that an awards framework would continue to exist, but it would be simplified, although it would continue as a benchmark for community standards about reasonable working conditions. Employers and employees would then be free to go off and negotiate their own enterprise agreements. The agreements would have to be signed off by the Industrial Arbitration Commission where they would have to pass a 'no-disadvantage' test when compared to the award. The same principle was applied when individual contracts were introduced. People no longer had to be on an award. Nor did they have to be a part of an enterprise agreement. They could strike up their own arrangements and sign their own personal contract as long as it was above the award.

On the surface the reforms offered the best of both worlds – protection and flexibility. But the reforms began a slow rot in the awards system. The new laws undermined the power base of the unions. As people moved into enterprise bargaining and individual contracts they became disconnected. They stopped associating their pay and conditions with union actions. They stopped becoming union members, stripping unions of their income stream and legitimacy. As the unions weakened their ability to uphold the awards was threatened. The system was set to slowly crumble.

In 1996 the Howard government came to power and accelerated the trend. Its first instalment was an extension of what had gone before. New laws further encouraged people to move towards enterprise agreements and one-on-one agreements. It also continued to take the old centralised safety net apart brick by brick.

It reduced the powers of the Industrial Arbitration Commission. It stripped back awards to 20 'allowable matters'. And it attacked the role of unions, putting restrictions on right of entry to workplaces and introducing penalties for industrial action.

In 2005 the Howard government used its control of the Senate to full advantage and slammed though the death knell of the old centralised wage arbitration system. It removed workers' right to collective bargaining. It mothballed the Industrial Arbitrations Commission. It froze the awards, and removed their status as a required minimum. It put five basic conditions in their place. There was now only a bare minimum safety net.

The laws were also a wholesale attack on the unions. They made it the boss' choice whether their workers are allowed to bargain as a group and involve unions. Even if the boss does decide they want to work with a union, the laws restrict the ways they can. The new laws make it illegal for employers and employees to agree to include any clauses in their contracts that:

- deal with pay deductions and payroll deduction facilities for trade union membership subscriptions or dues;
- allow employees to receive leave to attend union training sessions or paid leave to attend union meetings;
- allow persons bound by the workplace agreement to engage in or organise industrial action;
- deal with right of entry by unions and employer associations.

It represents a wholesale shift away from Australia's tradition of centralised wage arbitration.

Economic rationalists and WorkChoices

I am tentative about laying the new WorkChoices legislation at the feet of economic rationalists. Most economic rationalists aspire to having wages and conditions freely set by negotiation between two equal individuals. Yet the new laws are a long way from that ideal. The WorkChoices legislation aims to give employers absolute control over the wages and conditions of their workforce. John Howard made his intention clear: 'Now our position is very clear and that is that it's for the employer to determine the nature of the industrial arrangement in a workplace ...'

The new laws tilt the playing field in favour of employers. They do this through 687 pages of rules and regulations. They constrain what workers are and are not allowed to bargain on. Even Dr Nick Gruen, a former Commissioner from the notoriously economic rationalist Productivity Commission, conveyed his distaste for the laws:

> It is supposed to enhance workplace choices – but not if the government does not like your choice. You can swap two weeks leave for more cash, but you can't even offer to trade less cash for re-instatement of your current protections against unfair dismissal. If your union suggests it, it can be fined $33,000.

While many economic rationalists support de-regulation, this is not what they had in mind.

Many economic rationalists' attitudes to WorkChoices laws debunk the common assumption that economic rationalists are big business stooges. Economic rationalists' failure to put any weight on the power divide between the powerful and the powerless is often assumed to be a deliberate oversight. It is assumed they are rooting for the big end of town. In my experience that is not true. Most economic rationalists are well-meaning souls who simply have a particular vision of how to make Australia great. Their education simply overlooks the power divide. The recent reforms are one of those examples that put clear light of day between big business and economic rationalists.

Conclusion

The crux of the debates about industrial regulations systems is about values. People aspire to different systems because they have different beliefs about how the world works and what the system should deliver. They have differing views on the power divide between bosses and workers. They place varying weight on lifestyle versus the pay packet. And they have different views about the best way to manage workplace relationships.

The re-making of Australia's industrial relations system reflects a transformation in policy makers' worldviews and priorities. We have moved away from a centralised wage-fixing system that sought to even up the playing field and arbitrate conflict and that emphasised quality of life and protecting the vulnerable. We have moved to a system that tilts the playing field in favour of employers, outlaws conflict and assumes boosting business profits is the best way to meet everyone's needs.

John Howard is right when he argues that the transformation in industrial relations will change Australia forever.

Bibliography

ABC News (2006) *Tree of Knowledge Poisoned*, ABC News Online, 22 May. Retrieved 5 November 2006 from http://www. abc.net.au/westqld/stories/s1644052.htm

ACTU (1999) *Employment Security and Working Hours – A National Survey of Current Workplace Issues.* Melbourne, Australian Council of Trade Unions.

Akerlof, G. A. and R. E. Kranton (2000) 'Economics and Identity'. *Quarterly Journal of Economics* CXV: 717–53.

Appleyard, B. (1992) *Understanding the Present: Science and the Soul of Modern Man.* London, Pan Books.

Argy, F. (1998) *Australia at the Crossroads: Radical Free Market or Progressive Liberalism.* Sydney, Allen & Unwin.

—— (2003) *Where to from Here? Australian Egalitarianism under Threat.* Sydney, Allen & Unwin.

Australian Bureau of Statistics. Various publications.

Australian Chamber of Commerce and Industry (2005) *ACCI Modern Workplace: Modern Future Blueprint.* Retrieved 5 November 2006 from http://www.acci.asn.au/WRBluePrintMain.htm

—— (2005) *The Economic Case for Workplace Relations Reform: Position Paper.* Retrieved 5 November 2006 from http://www. acci.asn.au/text_files/Discussion%20Papers/Economic%20 Case%20for%20WR%20Reform%20Electronic%20Copy. pdf

Australian Council of Trade Unions (2005) *Submission to Senate Employment, Workplace Relations and Education Legislation Committee: Inquiry into the Workplace Relations Amendment (WorkChoices) Bill 2005.* Retrieved 5 November 2006 from http://www.aph.gov.au/Senate/committee/eet_ctte/wr_work choices05/submissions/sub171.pdf

Banfield, E. C. (1958) *The Moral Basis of a Backward Society.* Chicago, The Free Press.

Barro, R. J. and X. Sala-i-Martin (1999) *Economic Growth.* Cambridge, Mass., MIT Press.

Baumol, W. and W. Oates (1988) *The Theory of Environmental Policy.* Cambridge University Press.

Blandy, R. (2005) 'Labour Market Reform – What Needs to Be Done?' Anne Hawke Memorial Lecture, University of South Australia. Retrieved 5 November 2006 from http://www. henrythornton.com/article.asp?article_id=3674

Blinder, A. S. (1987) *Hard Heads, Soft Hearts: Tough-Minded Economics for a Just Society.* Reading, Mass., Addison-Wesley.

Bourdieu, P. (1985) 'The Forms of Capital', in J. G. Richardson (ed.), *Handbook of Theory and Research for the Sociology of Education.* New York, Greenwood, 241–58.

Bourdieu, P. and L. J. D. Wacquant (1992) *An Invitation to Reflexive Sociology.* Cambridge, UK, Polity Press.

Braithwaite, V. and R. Blamey (1998) 'Consensus, Stability and Meaning in Abstract Social Values'. *Australasian Political Studies Association* 33(3): 363–80.

Briggs, C. and J. Buchanan (2000) *Australian Labour Market Deregulation: A Critical Assessment.* Parliamentary Library Research Paper 21 1999–2000, Parliament of Australia.

Briggs, C., J. Buchanan and I. Watson (2006) *Wages Policy in an Era of Deepening Wage Inequality.* Occasional Paper 1/2006, Policy Paper #4, The Academy of the Social Sciences in Australia.

Business Council of Australia (1989) *Enterprise-Based Bargaining Units: A Better Way of Working.* Report by the Industrial Relations Study Commission, Business Council of Australia.

Callon, M. (1998) 'Introduction: The Embeddedness of Economic Markets', in M. Callon, *The Laws of the Markets.* Oxford, Blackwell.

Campbell, I. and P. Brosnan (1999) 'Labour Market Deregulation in Australia: The Slow Combustion Approach to Workplace Change'. *International Review of Applied Economics* 13(3): 353–94.

Carroll, J. and R. Manne (1992) *Shutdown: The Failure of Economic Rationalism and How to Rescue Australia.* Melbourne, Text Publishing Co.

Coleman, J. S. (1986) 'Social Theory, Social Research and a Theory of Action'. *American Journal of Sociology* (91): 1309–35.

—— (1990) *Foundations of Social Theory*. Cambridge, Mass., Belknap Press of Harvard University Press.

Coleman, J. S. and T. J. E. Fararo (1992) *Rational Choice Theory: Advocacy and Critique*. Newbury Park, CA, Sage Publications.

Conway, R. (1972) *The Great Australian Stupor: An Interpretation of the Australian Way of Life*. Melbourne, Sun Books.

Cooter, R. and R. Rappoport (1984) 'Were the Ordinalists Wrong about Welfare Economics?', *Journal of Economic Literature* XXII(June): 507–530.

Cox, E. (1995) *A Truly Civil Society*. Sydney, ABC Books.

—— (1997) 'Building Social Capital'. *Health Promotion Matters* 4.

—— (1998) 'Measuring Social Capital as Part of Progress and Well-being', in R. Eckersley (ed.), *Measuring Progress – Is Life Getting Better?* Melbourne, CSIRO Publishing, 157–68.

Deane, P. (1978) *The Evolution of Economic Ideas*. Cambridge, UK, Cambridge University Press.

Diamond, J. M. (1997) *Guns, Germs, and Steel: The Fates of Human Societies*. New York, W.W. Norton & Co.

Dobb, M. H. (1973) *Theories of Value and Distribution since Adam Smith: Ideology and Economic Theory*. Cambridge, UK, Cambridge University Press.

Eckersley, R. (1999) *Quality of Life in Australia: An Analysis of Public Perceptions*. Canberra, The Australia Institute.

Edwards, B. and M. W. Foley (1998) 'Social Capital and Civil Society beyond Putnam'. *American Behavioural Scientist* 42(2).

Edwards, J. J. K. (1996) *Keating: The Inside Story*. Ringwood, Vic., Viking.

Edwards, L. (2000) 'Bridging the Divide between GDP and Quality of Life', in Glover and Patmore, *Reclaiming Our Government for the People*, 31–42.

Edwards, M. and C. H. A. R. Miller (2001) *Social Policy, Public Policy: From Problem to Practice*. Sydney, Allen & Unwin.

Ferguson, M. (1993) 'Where Did Enterprise Bargaining Come from, What Is It and Where Is It Going'. President of ACTU's address to Enterprise Bargaining Seminar, Parliament House Adelaide, 23 February.

Foucault, M. (1967) *Madness and Civilization: A History of Insanity in the Age of Reason.* London, Tavistock.

—— (1970) *The Order of Things: An Archaeology of the Human Sciences.* New York, Pantheon Books.

—— (1976) *The Archaeology of Knowledge* (tr. A. M. Sheridan Smith). New York, Harper & Row.

Freebairn, J., M. Porter et al. (1987) *Spending and Taxing: Australian Reform Options.* Sydney, Allen & Unwin.

Friedman, M. (1962) *Capitalism and Freedom.* University of Chicago Press.

—— (1981) *The Invisible Hand in Economics and Politics.* Singapore, Institute of Southeast Asian Studies.

Friedman, M. and R. Friedman (1980) *Free to Choose: A Personal Statement.* Melbourne, Macmillan Company of Australia.

Frijters, P. and R. G. Gregory (2006) 'From Golden Age to Golden Age: Australia's "Great Leap Forward"?' *Economic Record* June: 207–24.

Fukuyama, F. (1992) *The End of History and the Last Man.* New York, Free Press.

—— (1995) *The Social Virtues and the Creation of Prosperity.* New York, Free Press.

—— (1995) *Trust: The Social Virtues and the Creation of Prosperity.* London, Hamish Hamilton.

Gabbitas, O. and D. Eldridge (1998) *Directions for State Tax Reform.* Canberra, Productivity Commission.

Galbraith, J. K. (1973) *Economics and the Public Purpose.* Boston, Houghton Mifflin.

—— (1991) *A History of Economics: The Past as the Present.* London, Penguin Books.

Geertz, C. (1973) *The Interpretation of Cultures: Selected Essays.* New York, Basic Books.

Gibson, K., J. Cameron et al. (1999) *Negotiating Restructuring: A Study of Regional Communities Experiencing Rapid Social and Economic Change.* Melbourne, Australian Housing and Urban Research Unit, Monash University.

Gittins, R. (2005) 'The Economics of WorkChoices'. Address to the Australian Business Economists' Annual Forecasting

Conference, Sydney. (see extracts at http://www.newmatilda.
com/policytoolkit/policydetail.asp?PolicyID=269&Categor
yID=16)

Glaeser, E., D. Laibson et al. (2000) 'Measuring Trust'. *Quarterly
Journal of Economics* CVX(3): 811–46.

Glover, D. and G. Patmore (2000) *New Voices for Social Democracy.*
Melbourne, Pluto Press and Australian Fabian Society.

—— (2000) *Reclaiming Our Government for the People: Labor
Essays 2001.* Melbourne, Pluto Press.

Goot, M. (2000) 'Politics, Politicians and the Parties: How Has
Public Opinion Changed and How Has It Remained the
Same?'. Parliament House Lecture Series.

Granovetter, M. (1985) 'Economic Action and Social Structure: The
Problem of Embeddedness'. *American Journal of Sociology*
91(3): 481–510.

Gregory, R. G. (2002) *Can This be the Promised Land? Work and
Welfare for the Modern Women.* Notes to accompany the
National Institute Public Lecture, Parliament House.

—— (2005) 'Australian Labour Markets, Economic Policy and My
Late Life Crisis', in J. Isaac and R. D. Lansbury (eds), *Labour
Market Deregulation, Rewriting the Rules.* Annandale, NSW,
The Federation Press, 204–20.

Gruen, N. (2006) 'Bad Economics and Bad Leadership', *On Line
Opinion*, 28 April. Retrieved 5 November 2006 from
http://www.onlineopinion.com.au/print.asp?article=3893

Hanson, P. as quoted in (2006) *Costello Accused of 'Islamophobia'*, ABC
Newsonline, February 24. Retrieved 5 November 2006 from
http://www.abc.net.au/news/newsitems/200602/s1577530.htm

Harding, A. (1996) *Recent Trends in Income Inequality. Dialogues on
Australia's Future.* Melbourne, Centre for Strategic Economic
Studies, Victoria University.

—— (2001) 'Overview of Social and Economic Impacts and
Emerging Trends'. Institute of Public Administration
Australia National Conference.

Harding, A. and H. Greenwell (2001) *Trends in Income and
Expenditure Inequality in the 1980s and 1990s.* Discussion Paper
No 56, Canberra, National Centre for Social and Economic
Modelling.

Headey, B. (1992) *Understanding Happiness: A Theory of Subjective Well-Being.* Melbourne, Longman Cheshire.

Heilbroner, R. (1995) 'Putting Economics in Its Place'. *Social Research* 62(4): 883–97.

Heilbroner, R. L. (1969) *The Worldly Philosophers: The Great Economic Thinkers.* London, Allen Lane.

—— (1973) 'Economics as a "Value-Free" Science'. *Social Research* Spring: 129–43.

Henry, K. and M. Derlet (1993) *Talking Up a Storm: Nine Women and Consciousness-Raising.* Sydney, Hale & Iremonger.

Hicks, J. R. (1939) *Capital and Value: An Inquiry into Fundamental Principles of Economic Theory.* Oxford, Oxford University Press.

Hirschman, A. O. (1977) *The Passions and the Interests: Political Arguments for Capitalism before Its Triumph.* Princeton University Press.

Horne, D. (1964) *The Lucky Country: Australia in the Sixties.* Ringwood, Vic., Penguin Books.

Howard, J. (2004) Address to the Liberal Party Western Australia State Council, Hyatt Hotel, Perth, 31 July. Retrieved 5 November 2006 from http://www.pm.gov.au/news/speeches/speech1040.html

—— (2006) Address to the Quadrant Magazine 50th Anniversary Dinner, Four Seasons Hotel, Sydney, 3 October.

Hutchinson, T. W. (1994) *The Uses and Abuses of Economics: Contentious Essays on History and Method.* London, Routledge.

Isaac, J. and R. D. Lansbury (2005) *Labour Market Deregulation: Rewriting the Rules.* Annandale, NSW, The Federation Press.

Jessop, B. (1999) 'The Social Embeddedness of the Economy and Its Implications for Economic Governance', in F. Adaman and P. Devine (eds), *The Socially Embedded Economy.* Montreal, Black Rose Books.

Jones, P. and J. Cullis (2000) '"Individual Failure" and the Analytics of Social Policy'. *Journal of Social Policy* 29(1): 73–93.

Kelly, P. (1994) *The End of Certainty: Power, Politics and Business in Australia.* Sydney, Allen & Unwin.

—— (1994) *The End of Certainty: The Story of the 1980s,* rev. edn. St Leonards, NSW, Allen & Unwin.

Kenyon, P. (1992) *Does Australia's Past Have a Useful Economics?* Murdoch, WA, Murdoch University.

Kingston, M. (1999) *Off the Rails: The Pauline Hanson Trip.* Sydney, Allen & Unwin.

Krugman, P. (1995) *Development, Geography and Economic Theory.* Cambridge, Mass., MIT Press.

Latham, M. (1998) *Civilising Global Capital: New Thinking for Australian Labor.* Sydney, Allen & Unwin.

—— (2001) 'Reinventing Collectivism: The New Social Democracy'. The Third Way Conference, Centre for Applied Economic Research, University of New South Wales, Sydney (reproduced by Crikey.com).

Leigh, A. (2005) 'Workers Solidarity, but Only for a Few', *On Line Opinion* 11 March. Retrieved 5 November 2006 from http://www.onlineopinion.com.au/view.asp?article=3232

Levinson, P. (1982) *In Pursuit of Truth: Essays on the Philosophy of Karl Popper on the Occasion of His 80th Birthday.* Atlantic Highlands, NJ, Harvester Press.

Levy-Garboua, L. (1979) *Sociological Economics.* London, Sage Publications.

Lewis, P. E. T. (2003) 'The Australian Labour Market: Some Social and Economic Consequences'. H. R. Nicholls Society Annual Conference, Melbourne, 2–4 May.

Lieblich, A., R. Tuval-Mashiach et al. (1998) *Narrative Research: Reading, Analysis and Interpretation.* Thousand Oaks, Sage Publications.

MacIntyre, A. (1985) *After Virtue: A Study in Moral Theory.* London, Duckworth.

Mackay, H. (1999) *The Mind and Mood of Australia '99.* Sydney, Mackay Research Pty Ltd.

—— (1999) *Turning Point: Australians Choosing Their Future.* Sydney, Pan Macmillan.

Mankiw, N. G., J. Gans and S. King (1999) *Principles of Microeconomics.* Sydney, Harcourt Brace Australia.

Marx, K. (1945) *Capital: A Critique of Political Economy.* Calcutta, Saraswaty Library.

—— (1967) *The Communist Manifesto.* Harmondsworth, Penguin.

Maslow, A. H. (1968) *Toward a Psychology of Being*, 2nd edn. Princeton, NJ, Van Nostrand.

McEwen, J. and D. Veitch (1996) *McEwen's Way*. Melbourne, David Syme College of National Economics, Public Administration & Business Ltd.

McGregor, C. (1966) *Profile of Australia*. London, Hodder and Stoughton.

McLean, G. F. (1998) 'Restorying the "Polis": Civil Society as Narrative Reconstruction – Call for Interest'. Conference paper, Washington, DC, Catholic University of America, Centre for Narrative Studies/Council for Research in Values and Philosophy, 3 September – 6 November.

McNutt, P. A. (1996) *The Economics of Public Choice*. Cheltenham, Edward Elgar.

McTaggart, D. (1996) *National Competition Policy: A Queensland Perspective*. Melbourne, Committee for Economic Development of Australia.

Meagher, G. and S. Wilson (2006) 'After Howard's Decade is Australia More Conservative?' Symposium on a Decade of Howard Government, Australian Review of Public Affairs Digest. Retrieved 5 November 2006 from http://www.australianreview.net/digest/2006/02/meagher_wilson. html

Mill, J. S. (1992) *On Liberty*. New York, Legal Classics Library.

Mills, S. (1993) *The Hawke Years: The Story from the Inside*. Ringwood, Vic., Viking.

Mohr, J. W. (1998) 'Measuring Meaning Structures'. *Annual Review of Sociology* 24: 345–70.

Morris, M. and P. Patton (1979) *Michel Foucault: Power, Truth, Strategy*. Sydney, Feral Publications.

National Competition Council (1999) *National Competition Policy: Some Impacts on Society and the Economy*. Canberra, AusInfo.

Nietzsche, F. W. (1911) *Beyond Good and Evil: Prelude to a Philosophy of the Future* (tr. H. Zimmern). Edinburgh, T. N. Foulis.

North, D. C. (1981) *Structure and Change in Economic History*. New York, Norton.

Office of Employment Advocate website (<see http://www.oea.gov.au/graphics.asp?showdoc=/employers/prohibited Content.asp>)

O'Neill, S., I. Kurrupu and B. Harris, *Workplace Reforms: A Chronology of Business, Community and Government Responses*. Parliamentary Library Publications, Parliament of Australia. Retrieved 5 November 2006 from http://www.aph.gov.au/library/pubs/online/WorkplaceRelations.htm

Ormerod, P. (1995) *The Death of Economics*. London, Faber and Faber.

—— (1998) *Butterfly Economics: A New General Theory of Social and Economic Behavior*. New York, Pantheon Books.

Oxley, A. (2000) *Seize the Future*. Sydney, Allen & Unwin.

Pack, H. and L. E. Westphal (1986) 'Industrial Strategy and Technological Change: Theory versus Reality'. *Journal of Development Economics* 22: 87–128.

Parham, D. (1999) *The New Economy?: A New Look at Australia's Productivity Performance*. Canberra, Commonwealth of Australia.

Parliamentary Library (2005) *Bills Digest No. 66 2005–06 Workplace Relations Amendment (Work Choices) Bill 2005*. Parliament of Australia. Retrieved 5 November 2006 from http://www.aph.gov.au/library/pubs/bd/2005-06/06bd066.htm

Peetz, D. (1998) *Unions in a Contrary World: The Future of the Australian Trade Union Movement*. New York, Cambridge University Press.

Pettit, P. (2001) 'The Virtual Reality of Homo Economicus'. *The Monist Volume* 73(3): 308–29.

Pigou, A. C. (1932) *The Economics of Welfare*, 4th edn. London, Macmillan and Co. (see <http://www.econlib.org/LIBRARY/NPDBooks/Pigou/pgEW.html>).

Polanyi, K. (1944) *The Great Transformation: The Political and Economic Origins of Our Time*. New York, Rinehart & Company.

Popay, J. (2000) 'Social Capital: The Role of Narrative and Historical Research'. *Journal of Epidemiology and Community Health* 54(6): 401.

Popper, K. (1987) *Evolutionary Epistemology, Rationality, and the Sociology of Knowledge*. La Salle, IL, Open Court.

Portes, A. (1998) 'Social Capital; Its Origins and Applications in Modern Sociology'. *Annual Review of Sociology* 24: 1–24.

Pringle, J. D. (1965) *Australian Accent.* London, Chatto and Windus.

Productivity Commission (1999) *Impact of Competition Policy Reforms on Rural and Regional Australia: Draft Report.* Canberra, Commonwealth of Australia.

—— (2000) *Microeconomic Reform and the Environment: Workshop Proceedings.* Melbourne, Productivity Commission.

—— (2001) *Structural Adjustment: Key Policy Issues.* Melbourne, Productivity Commission.

—— (2001) *Telecommunications Competition Regulation: Draft Report.* Belconnen, ACT, Productivity Commission.

Pusey, M. (1991) *Economic Rationalism in Canberra: A Nation-Building State Changes Its Mind.* Cambridge University Press.

Pusey, M. and N. Turnbull (2005) 'Have Australians Embraced Economic Reform?', in S. Wilson, R. Gibson, G. Meagher, D. Denemark & M. Western (eds), *Australian Social Attitudes: The First Report.* Sydney, UNSW Press, 161–81.

Putnam, R. D. (1993) 'The Prosperous Community: Social Capital and Public Life'. *The American Prospect* 4(13) (see <http://www.prospect.org/print-friendly/print/V4/13/putnam-r.html>).

Putnam, R. D., R. Leonardi et al. (1993) *Making Democracy Work: Civic Traditions in Modern Italy.* Princeton University Press.

Rawls, J. (1972) *A Theory of Justice.* Oxford University Press.

Reich, R. B. (1988) *The Power of Public Ideas.* Cambridge, Mass., Ballinger.

Ritzen, J. (2000) 'Social Cohesion, Public Policy and Economic Growth: Implications for OECD Countries', keynote address. The Contribution of Human and Social Capital to Sustained Economic Growth and Well-Being, Chateau Frontenac, Quebec City.

Ryan, M. (1995) *What Future for Payroll Taxes in Australia?* Canberra, Commonwealth Treasury.

Saul, J. R. (1997) *The Unconscious Civilization.* New York, Free Press.

Saulwick, I. (2006) *Stegley Lecture: Are Australians Becoming More Selfish? Does It Matter? (And if It Does What Can We Do About It?).* Hawthorn, Vic., Centre for Philanthropy and Social Investment, Swinburne University.

Saunders, P. (2003) *Examining Recent Changes in Income Equality in Australia.* Sydney, Social Policy Research Centre, University of New South Wales.

—— (2005) *Reviewing Trends in Wage Income Inequality.* Sydney, Social Policy Research Centre, University of New South Wales.

Sayer, A. (2000) 'Markets, Embeddedness and Trust: Problems of Polysemy and Idealism'. Research Symposium on Market Relations and Competition, University of Manchester.

Senate Legal and Constitutional References Committee (1998) *Legal Aid Report 3.* Canberra, Parliament of Australia.

Sheil, C. (2000) *Water's Fall: Running the Risks with Economic Rationalism.* Sydney, Pluto Press.

Simons, M. (1999) *Fit to Print: Inside the Canberra Press Gallery.* Sydney, University of New South Wales Press.

Smith, A. (1976) *An Inquiry into the Nature and Causes of the Wealth of Nations.* Oxford, Clarendon Press.

—— (1976) *The Theory of Moral Sentiments.* Oxford University Press.

Solow, R. M. (1970) *Growth Theory: An Exposition.* Oxford, Clarendon Press.

Stigler, G. J. (1965) *Essays in the History of Economics.* Chicago, University of Chicago Press.

Stilwell, F. J. B. (2000) *Changing Track: A New Political Economic Direction for Australia.* Sydney, Pluto Press.

Stuart Rees, G. R. and F. Stilwell (1993) *Beyond the Market: Alternatives to Economic Rationalism.* Sydney, Pluto Press.

Swedberg, R. (1991) 'Major Traditions of Economic Sociology'. *Annual Review of Sociology* 17: 251–76.

Tanner, L. (1999) *Open Australia.* Sydney, Pluto Press.

Tarrow, S. (1994) *Power in Movement: Social Movements, Collective Action and Politics.* Cambridge University Press.

—— (1996) 'Making Social Science Work across Space and Time: A Critical Reflection on Robert Putnam's *Making Democracy Work'. American Political Science Review* (June): 389–97.

Taylor, O. H. (1960) *A History of Economic Thought.* Tokyo, McGraw-Hill.

The Treasury (2006) *Australia's Century Since Federation at a Glance.* Retrieved 5 November 2006 from http://www.treasury. gov.au/documents/110/HTML/docshell.asp?URL=3round. asp

Tiffen, R. (2006) 'The Geoffrey Boycott of Australian Politics'. Symposium on a Decade of Howard Government, Australian Review of Public Affairs Digest. Retrieved 5 November 2006 from http://www.australianreview.net/digest/2006/02/tiffen. html

Tsumori, K. (2004) *How Union Campaigns on Hours and Casuals Are Threatening Low-Skilled Jobs.* Issue Paper No 44, Centre for Independent Studies.

Verikios, G. and Z. Xiao-guang (2001) *Global Gains from Liberalising Trade in Telecommunications and Financial Services.* Melbourne, Productivity Commission.

Viner, J. (1991) *Essays on the Intellectual History of Economics.* Princeton, Princeton University Press.

Ward, I. (1983) *Comparative Economic Systems: Theory and Practice.* Melbourne, Department of Economics, Monash University.

Wearing, A. and B. Headey (1998) 'Who Enjoys Life and Why: Measuring Subjective Well-being', in R. Eckersley (ed.), *Measuring Progress – Is Life Getting Better?* Melbourne, CSIRO Publishing, 169–82.

Weber, M. (1946) *From Max Weber: Essays in Sociology.* Translated, edited and introduction by H. H. Gerth and C. Wright Mills. New York, Oxford University Press.

Williams, P. (1997) *The Victory: The Inside Story of the Takeover of Australia.* Sydney, Allen & Unwin.

Wrong, D. (1961) 'The Oversocialized Conception of Man in Modern Sociology'. *American Sociological Review* 26: 183–93.

Young, I. M. (1990) *The Ideal of Community and the Politics of Difference. Feminism/Postmodernism.* New York, Routledge.

Index